**INTERNATIONAL
ENERGY AGENCY**

MW01273710

REGULATORY
INSTITUTIONS
IN LIBERALISED
ELECTRICITY
MARKETS

INTERNATIONAL ENERGY AGENCY

9, rue de la Fédération,
75739 Paris Cedex 15, France

The International Energy Agency (IEA) is an autonomous body which was established in November 1974 within the framework of the Organisation for Economic Co-operation and Development (OECD) to implement an international energy programme.

It carries out a comprehensive programme of energy co-operation among twenty-five* of the OECD's thirty Member countries.
The basic aims of the IEA are:

■ To maintain and improve systems for coping with oil supply disruptions;

■ To promote rational energy policies in a global context through co-operative relations with non-member countries, industry and international organisations;

■ To operate a permanent information system on the international oil market;

■ To improve the world's energy supply and demand structure by developing alternative energy sources and increasing the efficiency of energy use;

■ To assist in the integration of environmental and energy policies.

*IEA Member countries: Australia, Austria, Belgium, Canada, the Czech Republic, Denmark, Finland, France, Germany, Greece, Hungary, Ireland, Italy, Japan, Luxembourg, the Netherlands, New Zealand, Norway, Portugal, Spain, Sweden, Switzerland, Turkey, the United Kingdom, the United States. The European Commission also takes part in the work of the IEA.

ORGANISATION FOR ECONOMIC CO-OPERATION AND DEVELOPMENT

Pursuant to Article 1 of the Convention signed in Paris on 14th December 1960, and which came into force on 30th September 1961, the Organisation for Economic Co-operation and Development (OECD) shall promote policies designed:

■ To achieve the highest sustainable economic growth and employment and a rising standard of living in Member countries, while maintaining financial stability, and thus to contribute to the development of the world economy;

■ To contribute to sound economic expansion in Member as well as non-Member countries in the process of economic development; and

■ To contribute to the expansion of world trade on a multilateral, non-discriminatory basis in accordance with international obligations.

The original Member countries of the OECD are Austria, Belgium, Canada, Denmark, France, Germany, Greece, Iceland, Ireland, Italy, Luxembourg, the Netherlands, Norway, Portugal, Spain, Sweden, Switzerland, Turkey, the United Kingdom and the United States. The following countries became Members subsequently through accession at the dates indicated hereafter: Japan (28th April 1964), Finland (28th January 1969), Australia (7th June 1971), New Zealand (29th May 1973), Mexico (18th May 1994), the Czech Republic (21st December 1995), Hungary (7th May 1996), Poland (22nd November 1996), the Republic of Korea (12th December 1996) and Slovakia (28th September 2000). The Commission of the European Communities takes part in the work of the OECD (Article 13 of the OECD Convention).

FOREWORD

Regulation of the electricity supply industry in IEA countries is changing rapidly in response to market liberalisation. Though perfectly competitive markets would not need a sectoral regulator, many features of electricity markets continue to need regulation, and this will be true beyond the transitional phase of the newly competitive markets. Many new regulatory bodies have been established in the last few years and more are planned.

This book reviews the approaches to institutional reform taken by individual IEA countries. It describes the role, structure and procedures of electricity regulators, their relationship to government and to competition authorities. It considers the design issues that need to be addressed in establishing new regulatory bodies.

The book's key message is that institutional reform is fundamental to developing and sustaining a competitive electricity market. This does not mean that there is only one approach to institutional reform. National approaches vary reflecting different political traditions, although independent regulatory agencies are increasingly common. Whatever the approach, institutional reforms are important for neutrality and transparency in regulatory decision-making, so that competition between market players can flourish.

I would like to thank the Member countries of the IEA, and especially the IEA's Standing Group on Long-Term Co-operation, for their contributions to this book. The main author is Carlos Ocaña. Caroline Varley directed the work and provided editorial oversight. The book is published under my authority as Executive Director of the International Energy Agency.

Robert Priddle
IEA Executive Director

TABLE OF CONTENTS

1 INTRODUCTION AND SUMMARY 7

Institutional Reform is a Key Ingredient
of an Effective Reform Policy
Reasons for Change: Ensuring Impartiality and Transparency
The New Institutional Landscape of the ESI
There are Some Key Trends but also Large Institutional Diversity
Policy Implications
Structure of the Book

2 REGULATORY INSTITUTIONS 13

Defining Regulatory Institutions 13
Regulatory Independence 16
Designing Regulatory Agencies 19

3 COUNTRY REPORTS 31

Overview 31
Australia 40
Austria 45
Belgium 46
Canada 48
Czech Republic 52
Denmark 53
Finland 55
France 57
Germany 59
Greece 61
Hungary 62
Ireland 64
Italy 66
Japan 69

Luxembourg   71
Netherlands   72
New Zealand   74
Norway   76
Portugal   78
Spain   80
Sweden   82
Switzerland   84
Turkey   86
United Kingdom   87
United States   91

4 CONCLUSIONS   97

The Emergence of Independent Regulation   97
What do Independent Regulators have in Common?   99
Policy Implications   102

LIST OF BOXES

1. A Summary of the EU Framework   36
2. A Brief Annotated Bibliography   104
3. Regulatory Institutions in the Internet   106

LIST OF FIGURES

1. Budget of Regulatory Agencies   39
2. Staff of Regulatory Agencies   39

LIST OF TABLES

1. Key Design Options for Regulatory Agencies   19
2. Institutional Approaches of IEA Countries to ESI
       Regulation   33
3. Independent Regulatory Agencies in the ESI   34

INTRODUCTION AND SUMMARY

Institutional Reform is a Key Ingredient of an Effective Reform Policy

The reform of electricity markets encompasses a wide range of measures that go well beyond changing the regulation. Institutional reform – adapting regulatory institutions to their new roles and functions – is a key ingredient of effective reform. Institutional arrangements have a big impact on the quality and effectiveness of regulation[1] and, in particular, on shaping the incentives and expectations of firms, investors and consumers.

Previous studies in this series have dealt with the regulatory framework, the restructuring of the electricity supply industry and the introduction of consumer choice. This study surveys institutional reform.

Reasons for Change: Ensuring Impartiality and Transparency

The reasons for institutional change have to be seen in the context of other changes that are reshaping the electricity supply industry (ESI). Reformed markets require regulators to perform new tasks, such as ensuring open access to the electricity network, protecting the ability of consumers to choose their supplier, and enforcing antitrust laws. The expertise and means to carry out these tasks are often different from those required in the past.

---

1. *An analogy may help to understand why. There is little doubt that the success of commercial firms greatly depends on management and strategy. The fortunes of firms with similar corporate governance can be quite different depending on how they are managed. Despite that, the institutional arrangements on which a firm is built – transferable ownership, limited responsibility of owners – are also important determinants of performance because the incentives and expectations of owners, managers and third parties depend on these arrangements. Likewise, the governance of regulation can be expected to have an impact on regulatory performance even if the actual management of regulation, such as the actual decisions on prices, entry, or any other regulated aspect, has a more immediate and visible impact.*

Reformed markets require regulators to carry out their tasks impartially, without discrimination between market players. Regulators need to be independent from stakeholders and regulatory activities carried out as transparently as possible. To cope with these challenges institutional reform is generally needed.

The New Institutional Landscape of the ESI

The institutional framework of the ESI is already changing in response to these challenges. In most OECD countries several institutions share authority over the industry. Three institutions that are frequently present are "line ministries", regulatory agencies separated to some extent from the line ministry, and competition authorities. In federal countries these institutions may exist at both the federal and state levels of government. In the last decade, many new regulatory agencies have been set up around the world to oversee network industries such as electricity, gas supply and telecommunications either separately or together. The line ministry can be specialised in energy matters, or may have wider responsibilities for all industrial policy or for all economic policy.

The co-existence of several regulatory institutions with authority over the ESI raises a number of issues including:

- the autonomy and independence of each institution;
- the allocation of (possibly overlapping) responsibilities to each institution;
- the creation of co-ordination mechanisms among them;
- the governance and management of each institution (the question of collegial vs. one-person regulatory agencies).

This book describes how IEA countries are addressing these four issues. It reviews the main institutions involved in the regulation of the ESI, their roles and co-ordination in Australia, Austria, Belgium, Canada, the Czech Republic, Denmark, Finland, France, Germany, Greece, Hungary, Ireland, Italy, Japan, Luxembourg, the Netherlands,

New Zealand, Norway, Portugal, Spain, Sweden, Switzerland, Turkey, the UK and the US.

Emphasis is on the role and attributes of regulatory agencies and how they interact with ministries, competition authorities and other institutions. No attempt is made to compare the different models or to identify "best practices" in electricity regulation. Such an exercise is difficult to perform, particularly at this early stage, when many institutions are either quite young or subject to further change, but also because of the different legal and political traditions of OECD countries.

There are three broad institutional approaches to ESI regulation:

- Independent regulatory agencies separate from the ministry have been established in Australia, Canada, Denmark, Finland, France, Ireland, Italy, Portugal, Sweden, UK, and the US. These agencies often cover both gas and electricity, are responsible, among other matters, for network regulation, are governed by a collegial board, and operate on the basis of public consultation and other procedures meant to enhance transparency. In federal countries there are often regulators at the federal and state level with the former specialising in wholesale electricity trade and transmission and the latter concentrating on retail trade and distribution.

- In another large group of countries, ministries handle most regulatory responsibilities directly. This is the approach currently taken in Austria, Belgium, the Czech Republic, Germany, Greece, Japan, Luxembourg, New Zealand, Spain, Switzerland, and Turkey. In three of these countries – Belgium, Luxembourg and Spain – an independent advisory agency assists the ministry and a similar approach will be implemented in Greece. The actual role of ministries in regulation largely depends on the regulatory framework. For instance, there is less ministerial involvement in regulation, because there is less regulation, in countries with a negotiated approach to access and pricing, such as Germany and New Zealand.

- A third group of countries has established ministerial regulatory agencies. These are subordinated to the ministry but designed to operate autonomously in the day-to-day management of regulatory affairs. The scope of their activity is similar to that of independent agencies. This is the approach adopted in Hungary, the Netherlands, and Norway. The Czech Republic plans to establish an autonomous ministerial agency by 2001.

There are Some Key Trends but also Large Institutional Diversity

Independent regulatory agencies share a number of strategic elements, such as safeguards to protect their independence, a procedural approach based on openness, transparency and consultation, and an emphasis on economic, as opposed to social or environmental, regulation. Beyond these general similarities, however, regulatory institutions are largely country-specific.

Variations in the institutional framework arise partly from different legal and political traditions. They also reflect the need for institutional frameworks to be consistent with regulatory practice and industry structure. The adoption of a particular institutional framework is generally linked to the regulatory model that is being implemented. Regulatory agencies tend to be stronger in countries in which structural such as unbundling policies are heavily emphasized. More regulatory involvement is required to monitor and enforce unbundling regulations.

Diversity also reflects different compromises among the many goals that the institutions aim to meet. These include specific regulatory goals such as transparency, protection against the capture of regulators by industry interests and short-term political pressure, the predictability and stability of regulation, accountability, and keeping down red tape. There are also managerial goals, such as cost efficiency and flexibility. Variations in the institutional framework may also reflect the newness of ESI reforms. Regulatory institutions in telecommunications, which has being undergoing reforms for a longer period, show a larger degree of convergence than those in electricity[2].

Policy Implications

Changes in ESI regulatory institutions are generating increased transparency and independence but also complexity. Governments need to ensure that the policies of the various regulatory institutions are mutually consistent and take a "whole-of-government" approach to minimise the cost of regulation for stakeholders.

Evolutionary changes in the relative weight of energy, regulatory and competition policies need to be reflected in the resources allocated to each task. Regulatory needs are quickly changing as competition develops, Electricity supply increasingly crosses national boundaries and electricity and gas are becoming increasingly integrated. The institutional framework needs periodic review to reflect these trends.

Close monitoring of experience in other countries and, whenever possible, benchmarking of regulatory institutions is important in settling the various issues that remain open. These include the need for political independence of regulators, defining the jurisdiction and functions of regulatory agencies, and promoting their co-ordination with other institutions. New institutional settings are progressively being developed, tested and refined in a number of countries.

Structure of the Book

Chapter 2 defines the different institutions involved in the ESI and examines the main design options for independent regulatory agencies. A survey of IEA countries is provided in chapter 3. This

---

2. See *"Telecommunications Regulations: Institutional Structures and Responsibilities"*. OECD *DSTI/ICCP/TISP(99)15/FINAL. 25 May 2000.*

suggests a number of trends in the design of regulatory agencies, and these are discussed in chapter 4, together with a review of some open issues in the choice of institutional framework, and an analysis of policy implications.

REGULATORY INSTITUTIONS

Defining Regulatory Institutions

The key players, those with actual regulatory powers, are ministries, independent regulatory agencies and competition authorities. Other organisations without formal "final" powers but with a potentially significant role, include ministerial agencies and independent advisory bodies.

■ "Economic" and "Social" Regulators

It is customary to distinguish between "economic" regulation and "social" regulation. Economic regulation is industry specific. It deals with prices, quality and reliability, market entry and exit, and investment. Social regulation, on the other hand, aims to protect a social interest such as health, safety and the environment. Economic regulation is primarily concerned with correcting the outcome of monopolistic or imperfectly competitive markets. Social regulation is primarily concerned with correcting externalities or information problems.

Typically, "economic" and "social" regulations are managed by separate organisations. Environmental protection is often the responsibility of ministries and regulatory agencies that are not responsible for either energy policy or energy regulation[3]. One exception to this separation of tasks concerns technical areas that require detailed industry knowledge like air safety and reliability standards. The specialisation of regulatory institutions reflects the different nature of the issues and the different tools applied to deal with them.

This book focuses on regulators with a specific mandate to regulate the ESI. In practice, this generally means those responsible for economic regulation. Institutions with no specific ESI

---

3. There are, however, exceptions as Denmark. See chapter 3.

responsibility, including most environmental agencies, are not covered.

■ Ministries and Ministerial Agencies

A line ministry, if there is one, is the part of the executive branch of government that is specifically responsible for the industry. The ministry responsible for electricity matters is often the ministry of industry or the ministry of economics. However, in a few OECD countries, a separate energy ministry exists. Autonomous ministerial agencies linked to the line ministry have been set up in some countries. These institutions operate on a separated budget and under an autonomous management and may be subject to a differentiated legal framework (civil service regulations may not apply) but are ultimately subordinated to the ministry. In practice, however, autonomous ministerial agencies in some countries operate with a substantial degree of independence.

■ Independent Regulatory Agencies

Independent agencies are defined as independent public bodies empowered to regulate specific aspects of an industry; they are not merely consultative or advisory bodies. They share regulatory activities with other public entities, notably the ministry, and are isolated, to some extent, from short-term political influence[4]. The functions of these agencies often include the regulation of network access and pricing, and end-user tariffs. Regulatory agencies may have judicial or quasi-judicial powers like setting fines and penalties for non-compliance or acting as an arbitrator in disputes among industry participants. Some agencies also have an explicit mandate to protect end-users and to regulate entry and exit through the issue of licences.

Different types of independent agency are possible depending both on the degree of political independence and on the range of powers assigned to them. Many different combinations of political independence and regulatory powers can be found in practice.

---

4. *Regulatory independence is further discussed below.*

In addition to being endowed with independence and concrete powers, independent regulatory agencies split regulatory activities with the line ministry. In theory at least, the "division of labour" between ministry and regulatory agency allocates policy making – setting the general framework and rules – to the line-ministry. Implementation of these rules is the responsibility of the regulatory agency. However, the frontier between policy and regulation is often blurred and there is some overlap[5].

Regulatory agencies are, to some extent, superimposed on the three traditional branches of government: executive, legislative and judicial. The split and possible overlap of regulatory activities may indeed be one of the key benefits of setting up regulatory agencies. It has been argued that the co-existence of two or more regulatory institutions may result in more effective monitoring. It may also reduce the scope for capture of the regulators by industry interests[6]. On the other hand, the existence of many regulatory institutions increases the complexity of regulatory processes, and requires the development of appropriate co-ordination mechanisms.

■ Independent Advisory Agencies

In a number of countries there are independent advisory agencies. These are independent from the ministry. They operate autonomously, the appointment of the regulators cannot be revoked and perform an advisory role in a wide variety of regulatory issues but have no decision-making powers on regulatory matters. They usually have monitoring responsibilities and authority in the resolution of disputes on such issues as network access.

■ Competition Authorities

The competition authority is the institution or set of institutions in charge of enforcing competition law. Competition authorities have

---

5. Indeed, in some countries, like the UK, the jurisdictional competencies of ministry and regulatory agencies are set to overlap in that the agreement of both institutions is required for some key decisions.

6. See J.J. Laffont and D. Martimort (1999) (Box 2).

two functions. They act *ex post* to enforce prohibitions on collusion, abuse of a dominant position and other anti-competitive behaviour. They may act *ex ante* to prevent mergers and acquisitions which are deemed to be detrimental to competition. They may also apply structural remedies such as mandated divestitures when the structure of the industry is judged to block competition. By contrast, regulatory authorities primarily act *ex ante*, setting rules that frame the conduct of market participants. There is significant overlap between regulatory and competition agencies in many areas including network access and pricing, and structural policies such as the unbundling of generation and end-user supply, mergers and divestitures.

Regulatory Independence

■ Independence from Stakeholders

A regulator can be independent in two ways: politically independent and independent from stakeholder interests. The latter means that regulated parties have limited influence on regulatory decisions. This is necessary to ensure that regulation is fair and does not favour one group of stakeholders over the others. Virtually all approaches to regulation are based on the principle that regulators should not be "captured" by the interests of industry players. However, capture may result from a number of factors, including insufficient regulatory authority and informational asymmetries[7]. For instance, companies are typically better informed than regulators concerning costs and technology and this may reduce the ability of the regulators to set prices.

In order to avoid regulatory capture, regulators are often subject to constraints on their relationship with the regulated parties during and after their tenure. These constraints apply regardless of whether the regulator is a ministry or a regulatory agency.

---

7. *A situation in which the utilities are better informed than the regulators in areas such as their costs and their future technological possibilities.*

Measures to support independence from stakeholders include a prohibition on regulators having a financial interest in the industry or working for it during or after their appointment as regulators. Selection procedures for regulators may also enhance independence. For instance, owners and employees of electricity utilities may not be eligible for regulatory appointments. Procedural norms to ensure transparency of decision making and to limit regulatory discretion also reinforce independence.

■ Political Independence: Definition

Political independence means that regulators are shielded from short-term political influence. The need for political independence is not an undisputed principle, even though it has gained considerable support in recent years. It is achieved through irrevocable mandates and other measures such as separate budgets, autonomy in the management of human resources and salaries, and non-renewable appointments. The actual scope of political independence depends not only on which of these measures are adopted but also on the powers of the regulatory agency. When an agency has broad powers, political independence has significant implications for the regulatory framework and the structure of industry. When regulatory agencies are limited to technical issues or advisory functions, the implications of political independence are less significant. In independent regulatory agencies regulators have irrevocable mandates.

■ Political Independence: Pros and Cons

Political independence serves three goals. First, it reduces the influence of short-term political pressures on regulation. There is general agreement that regulatory policies should not generally depend on short-term political circumstances. For instance, electricity prices should not be used as a tool to control inflation. Second, political independence may reinforce the independence of the regulator from special interest groups. Third, when the electricity companies are state-owned, political independence is required to avoid conflicts of interest between the state as owner and as regulator.

Despite these advantages, complete political independence is difficult to achieve both in principle and in practice[8]. In a democratic system legislative powers reside with elected bodies such as parliament. This means that, even if the regulator is politically independent, regulation is always subject to some political control and influence. In the US, where regulatory commissions are politically independent and have broad powers, market reform has prompted an increase in legislative activity in areas that were traditionally handled by the commissions. Complete independence may not be desirable, at least in certain circumstances, because it may result in a higher propensity to regulatory capture. A small and specialised industry regulator may find it difficult to counterbalance the influence of industry on public opinion, sustain a prolonged conflict with the industry or even attract staff with specialised technical skills.

In practice, regulators have to be nominated by some political institution, usually parliament, and thus political preferences will be reflected to some degree in the choice of regulators. This influence will be stronger the shorter the term of appointment. Even if regulators aim to act objectively, regulators can be sensitive to political circumstances. The personality and preferences of regulators matter in determining to what degree the regulatory process is actually affected by political circumstances.

The move towards political independence has implications for the management of the public sector because it usually entails setting up a separate organisation. This is costly and, more importantly, establishing autonomous organisations may produce some problems in the long term because of the tendency of organisations to grow and self-perpetuate. The policy implications of these managerial challenges are discussed in the conclusions.

8. Political independence is discussed in W. Smith (1996) "Utility Regulators: the Independence Debate" (See Box 2), P. Spiller (1996) "Institutions and Commitment" (See Box 2), and R. Noll (1971) "Reforming Regulation: An Evaluation of the Ash Council Proposals" (The Brookings Institution, Studies in the Regulation of Economic Activity, Staff Papers).

To summarise, regulatory independence from short-term political pressure promotes effective regulatory performance. However, some political control (and, thus, influence) over regulatory structures is both necessary and unavoidable. In the end, the issue of political independence is one of degree.

Designing Regulatory Agencies

Regulatory agencies can be designed in many different ways. Options include the role (or "mission") they are assigned, their governance, the specific regulatory functions and processes, the resources and internal management of the agency, the start-up strategy and other factors. The main options are discussed below.

■ Objectives

The goals of regulatory agencies are generally restricted to economic issues. Two common goals in the ESI and other network industries are protecting users and protecting investors. Users need to be protected from abuse by firms with substantial market power, while investors require protection from arbitrary action by government, such as setting tariffs that are not financially sustainable. Typically, regulatory agencies have to balance these two objectives. For instance, prices are set with the aim of protecting users from monopolistic pricing while allowing investors to recover their investments and earn a return on them. Regulatory agencies may be endowed with more general goals, such as promoting economic efficiency or market-oriented reforms. Institutions specifically serving these goals may be useful, especially since the greatest impediment to enhanced competition in many key sectors of the economy are often restrictions imposed by government laws and regulations[9]. Regulatory agencies do not generally have social goals. These are typically pursued by other institutions such as environmental agencies and ministries.

---

9. See Rauf Gonenc, Maria Maher and Giuseppe Nicoletti (2000): The Implementation and the Effects of Regulatory Reform: Past Experience and Current Issues. OECD Economics Department Working Paper No. 251.

Table 1

Key Design Options for Regulatory Agencies

Area	Design Issue	Key Options
Mission	Objectives	• One or several among: consumer protection investor protection economic efficiency competition advocacy
	Jurisdiction (powers)	• Regulatory powers only or, additionally: − mergers − other competition law − policy on entry, investment, privatisation
	Industry coverage	• One industry (ESI) or multi industry
Governance	Decision-making structure	• Single regulator or commission • Odd or even number of commissioners • Staggered terms or not
	Appointment of regulators	• Made by parliament or by government • Stakeholders allowed or not • Based on professional competence criteria or not
	Independence safeguards	• Irrevocable mandates • Prohibition of conflicts of interest during and after mandate • Stable funding
Regulatory activities	Functions	• One or several among: regulation of monopolies end-user tariffs and quality standards monitoring dispute resolution advisory role to government
	Process and appeals	• Process based on: − rule-making − negotiation among stake holders − monitoring and remedial action

Area	Design Issue	Key Options
Regulatory activities		• Rules to promote transparency of decision making such as hearings and publication of decisions • Designation of an independent appeals body or not • Grounds for appeal restricted to complaints on undue process or not
	Co-ordination with other authorities	• Formal or informal mechanisms for consultation and referral
Resources, Management and External Control	Funding	• Earmarked or not • From state budget or from industry • Size • Stability of time horizon
	Human resources	• Salaries at market levels or subject to civil service rules • Competence and specialisation of staff • Use of external resources
	Reporting and auditing	• Reporting to parliament, to line ministry, to other ministry • External audits
Transition Issues	Start-up Strategy	• Timing: set up before or after reform • Initially, staff on secondment from industry or ministry allowed or not

■ Jurisdiction and Powers

In addition to regulatory functions, regulatory agencies may be endowed with responsibility for other areas of public activity. The regulator can be assigned responsibilities in the implementation of merger policy and other aspects of competition law. These responsibilities may range from assisting competition authorities to carry out their duties, such as monitoring the market, reporting on suspected breaches of the law and providing advice on the decisions and remedies, to assuming the leading role in the enforcement of competition law. In the latter case, the regulator and the competition authority merge into one single institution.

The main arguments for keeping the regulator and the competition authority separate are that regulation and competition policy are different activities requiring different knowledge and specialization. In particular, separation favors the specialization of the regulator in one industry. On the other hand, merging regulatory and competition authorities can provide the industry watchdog with a more powerful set of tools to achieve its goals. Where the two entities are separate, which is the case in most countries, regulatory agencies usually have a role in assisting the competition authority or complementing its actions.

Regulatory agencies may also have a role in policy issues such as regulating entry and investment, or setting privatisation plans. The role of regulators is most often advisory. When executive powers are allocated to the regulator, these powers are concurrent with those of the ministry[10].

■ Industry Coverage

Regulatory agencies may deal with just one industry, like the ESI, a sector such as energy, or several sectors as in the case of network industries. The main advantages of multi-industry regulators are:

- Savings from shared activities, such as information collection and administration. In assessing the importance of these savings an important factor is the size of the industry to be regulated. In a small country it may be prohibitively costly to set up several industry-specific agencies while the impact of any foregone economies of scale is diluted when the economy is large.

- Reduced risk of regulatory capture or undue political influence, because of the reduced dependency of the agency on any particular industry or group.

- Avoidance of distortions in the investment of the regulated firms induced by regulatory inconsistencies across industries particularly when the activities concerned are substitutes as in the case of electricity and gas.

- Dealing with blurred industry boundaries, such as regulated companies with interests in both electricity and gas.

---

10. For example, the licensing of generation in the UK requires agreement by both the ministry and the regulator.

- Using knowledge gained from one industry in a related industry, as would be the case in regulating third-party access in several network industries.

On the other hand, industry-specific regulators may have the advantage of greater specialization and focus. It has also been argued that they are less likely to engage in socially wasteful discretionary behavior because they have less powers and information. Also, industry-specific regulators have advantages in terms of implementation in that they allow for experimentation, and the impact of any eventual failure is more limited. Finally, industry-specific regulators may be more effective when the regulation of the different industries differs widely, as when there is an open electricity industry and a heavily regulated gas industry.

■ Decision-making Structure

Decision-making can be assigned to a commission or to just one person. A commission is probably better insulated from conflicts of interests and regulatory capture in that it reflects multiple perspectives. However, this potential also constitutes a risk, as there may be pressure for a commission to be appointed to reflect a range of political views or to represent the interests of various stakeholders. A commission can also be more stable than a one-person body if the terms of the commissioners are staggered. A one-person regulator, on the other hand, has the advantages of being more clearly accountable and predictable, making decisions faster and being more economical. Virtually all agencies have an odd number of commissioners to prevent ties in voting. The number of commissioner ranges from 3 to 7 in most countries.

■ Appointment of Regulators

The professional and personal qualities of the commissioners are widely regarded as a key factor in the performance and independence of regulatory agencies. This is illustrated by a number of cases in which changes in the composition of an agency have significantly affected its stance on key issues such as price levels, restructuring and competition. Thus, the same legal framework may yield quite different results depending on the personality and preferences of the regulators.

Integrity, competence, the ability to exercise independent judgement, and the strength to resist pressure are indispensable for a regulator, while technical experience in the regulated industry is generally considered of secondary importance. Stakeholders are often excluded from the selection process as a means to avoid conflicts of interest and protect independence. The appointment can be made by parliament or by government or, in a number of countries, confirmed by parliament following a nomination by the government.

■ Independence Safeguards

Many devices can be used to protect the independence of regulators. Commissioners are usually appointed for a fixed and renewable term, of up to seven years, and, more rarely, have an indefinite term in office. The mandates are irrevocable, that is to say, governments have no discretion to shorten the term of appointment; removal from office may only occur under certain circumstances such as mental incapacity or proven corruption. In addition, there are provisions to avoid conflicts of interest during and after mandate. These include a ban on holding a financial interest in the regulated companies or working for them after leaving office (to avoid the so-called "revolving doors") or receiving any other form of compensation from these companies. There are other measures which aim to reduce the vulnerability of regulatory agencies to capture, including provisions to ensure a stable and reliable funding and exemption of salaries from civil service rules, thus allowing salaries to be competitive with those in the private sector.

■ Regulatory Functions

A large set of regulatory and related functions can be assigned to a regulatory agency including:

■ the regulation of monopolies (unbundling, network pricing and access conditions, rules for system operation and reliability);

- end-user tariffs;
- quality and performance standards;
- monitoring of market behaviour and performance;
- enforcement of rules;
- regulation of entry (licensing and authorisations);
- advising the government; and
- dispute resolution.

The actual allocation of functions depends both on the regulatory framework (what is regulated?) and on the institutional structure (how regulatory functions are divided among the agency, ministry and others?). There is a wide array of possibilities. Regulatory functions may be assigned exclusively to one organisation or, less frequently, concurrently to two or more organisations; licences may require the approval of both the ministry and the regulatory agency. Legislative bodies can change regulation by passing new laws. Legislative action to change the rules should be exceptional since legislation aims for stability. However, there has been much legislative action affecting the ESI in recent years, reflecting ongoing reforms. Some patterns in the allocation of functions to regulatory agencies are identified and discussed in chapter 4.

Regulatory functions can be allocated according to their "economic" or "social" nature. In this case the industry regulator typically has responsibility for economic regulation dealing with imperfect competition or monopolies or may be further restricted to cover only monopolies. Less frequently, regulatory agencies may have some responsibility for social regulation including distributional issues such as alleviating "fuel poverty" by facilitating access to basic energy services to low income households. Regulatory functions may also be allocated in a way which ensues the organisation that makes the rules does not enforce them. Separation of rule-making from rule implementation is intended to avoid conflicts of interest. It is also intended to underline the fact that setting the policy framework is a more "political" process than applying the rules once the framework is established. In practice, however, it is difficult to draw the line between the two.

In countries with a federal structure, an additional issue is the sharing of responsibilities between federal and state regulators. Federal regulation has the advantage that it is uniform. This is more efficient than a state by state approach when electricity markets do not conform to state boundaries. It also benefits from the fact that federal agencies have access to more information and avoid duplication of regulatory processes. On the other hand, state regulation allows for experimentation with different approaches and fosters innovation. If industry conditions vary from state to state, decentralised regulation may allow for adaptation of policies to local conditions. In practice, the responsibilities of federal and state regulators vary greatly reflecting the degree of decentralisation of policy-making in each country. Responsibilities of state regulators generally include the regulation of activities with a relatively small impact on other states, such as distribution and retail supply, while the responsibilities of federal regulators generally include the regulation of activities with a broader impact, such as interstate and international electricity trade.

■ Regulatory Process and Appeals

Process can focus on the elaboration of ex ante regulations by the regulatory agency. In this case, the process aims to provide guarantees of impartiality and fairness to stakeholders. As a result, it tends to be explicitly regulated and formal. Alternatively, process can focus on reaching consensus among stakeholders. In this case it tends to be less formal. It can be based on a more light-handed approach in which the role of regulators is primarily to monitor the industry and to take remedial action as needed. All regulatory systems combine, to some degree, all three approaches[11]. Some procedural approaches are better suited for some regulatory functions than for others. For instance, a consensus-building

---

11. See Wirick (1999): "New Models of Regulatory Commission Performance: The Diversity Imperative". National Regulatory Research Institute, Working Paper 99-15.

approach may be appropriate for the development of technical and operational rules, while setting the allowed revenue for a regulated monopoly may require a more formal, "quasi-judicial" procedure. Some systems rely more heavily on an *ex ante* approach, like that of the US, while others, like the Finnish, rely more heavily in monitoring and ex post remedies.

All independent regulatory agencies are subject to rules that promote transparency and predictability and provide an opportunity for stakeholders to present their views and to challenge the views of the agency. These include hearings and meetings of consultative committees before decisions are made and the publication of decisions and supporting reasoning once they are taken. In some systems these procedures are of a quasi-judicial nature, while in others processes are less formal. In addition, all systems provide for an appeal process conducted either by an independent appeals body or by a government body. Grounds for appeal may be restricted to factual errors or procedural mistakes. This ensures that the appeals body cannot overturn the judgement of the regulator. Alternatively, the merits of the decision can be reviewed by the appeals body. In this case, the independence of the regulator is effectively limited. In the design of the regulatory process there is nearly always a tradeoff between predictability and reduced regulatory risk on the one hand, and simplicity and cost effectiveness, on the other. As a general rule, a more formalised process reduces regulatory risk but requires more resources, such as legal advisors and auditors.

■ Co-ordination

As the number of regulatory bodies that cover the ESI grows, there is an increasing need to co-ordinate their actions. A concerted "whole-of-government" approach seems necessary to avoid the inefficiency of having "to deal with the different organisations that make up part of the regulatory jigsaw"[12]. Co-ordination helps both

---

12. *Utility Regulators Forum (1999), see Box 2.*

to ensure consistency and to reduce the costs borne by stakeholders who have to deal with several authorities and comply with their regulations. Co-ordination may be based on formal rules, requiring consultation, referral or information sharing on certain issues, or on informal co-operation arrangements.

■ Funding

Adequate human and financial resources are essential for an effective management of regulatory issues. Regulatory agencies usually operate with a separate budget approved by either government or parliament. This ensures a certain degree of autonomy in the agency's management. Funds can be obtained from general taxation through the national budget or, more frequently, from specific charges imposed on industry participants, such as charges on end-users or on the use of network services. In the latter case, funds may also be allocated through the national or state budget to increase transparency and to facilitate control. The size of the budget is important for performance. Too few resources compromise the ability of the agency to carry out its tasks. Too many resources may result in a lack of focus in agency activities in addition to wasting scarce public resources. The stability of funding over several budget periods is also important to allow for efficient management, as well as to safeguard independence as discussed above.

■ Human Resources

The challenges posed by the management of human resources in regulatory agencies are similar to those in other public organisations but ensuring the competence and specialisation of staff is particularly important. Regulatory agencies demand quite specialised skills and compete for them with industry. As a result, salaries are often set at market levels and are exempt from civil service compensation rules. In addition, regulatory agencies often use external consulting services to procure certain services and draw on specialised training programs, particularly during the start-up phase.

■ Reporting and Auditing

A number of mechanisms are designed to make the management of regulatory agencies accountable. Most agencies report to parliament or to a ministry which can be the line ministry or not. They are also subject to audits and other controls, generally in line with the procedures applied to other public organisations.

■ Start-up Strategy

Some transitional issues arise at the time of creating a regulatory agency. The timing of the agency set-up, either before or after reform, has an impact on the perception of reforms by stakeholders and determines the role of the agency in setting the regulatory framework. Start up funding, particularly if the agency's founding precedes reforms, may be provided by a government allocation. Temporary staff on secondment from industry or ministry may provide specialised skills not available elsewhere.

■ Other Issues

Another aspect of the design of regulatory agencies is the interaction with other institutions and with stakeholders. Formal procedures may be established to regulate the relationship with ministries, competition authorities and other institutions. Regulation may be governed by detailed procedures to determine the obligations and rights of stakeholders ("regulation by contract") or it may be based on more general rules. These legal matters are largely determined by the administrative and legal systems of each country.

COUNTRY REPORTS

Overview

This section reviews regulatory institutions in the power sector of IEA countries. Topics covered include the split of activities among ministries, regulatory agencies and competition authorities, sectors covered by the regulatory agency, governance and the size and budget of the regulatory agency. Emphasis is on the role of regulatory agencies and their interaction with governments. A more detailed account of the institutional framework is provided for countries in which one or several regulatory agencies have been set up. A brief summary of the regulatory framework is also provided for each country. The internal organisation of governments, including how responsibilities are allocated to the ministries, is not considered here. Instead, emphasis is on the role of governments vis-a-vis other institutions.

Within the European Union, the EU directive on the internal electricity market provides a common set of rules that applies to the regulatory framework and to the application of competition law. The directive does not make any explicit provisions for institutional change other than the need to provide a dispute resolution authority to deal with third-party access issues. This set of rules is summarised in Box 1 below.

■ Summary of National Approaches

Countries show a large variety of institutional approaches:

- In some countries, an independent agency shares regulatory responsibilities with the ministry. The split of powers between the different institutions varies:
  - the role of independent (federal or state) agencies vis-a-vis ministries, which is largest in the US, the United Kingdom, Canada and Australia;

- the powers attributed to independent agencies in other countries vary from the relatively large powers of the Italian regulator to the more specialised roles of the Finnish, Swedish, Portuguese, French and Danish agencies.

■ In other countries the line ministry has ultimate responsibility for most regulatory tasks. This approach is implemented in three different ways depending on the role of the ministry. Management of day-to-day affairs can be delegated to a ministerial agency or conducted directly by the ministry. In the latter case, there may be an independent advisory body to the ministry, or not. Independent advisory agencies are also responsible for dispute resolution, as discussed above. All three forms of ministry regulation are present in the IEA:

- a ministerial agency, intended to be largely independent in the management of day-to-day regulatory affairs, exist in Hungary, the Netherlands and Norway. The Czech Republic plans to establish an autonomous ministerial agency by 2001;

- an independent advisory agency that provides advice to the ministry and is responsible for dispute resolution exists in Belgium, Luxembourg and Spain. Greece is currently implementing a similar approach. In these countries, the ministry is directly involved in the management of day-to-day regulatory affairs;

- the ministry conducts all regulatory affairs in Austria, the Czech Republic, Germany, Japan, New Zealand, Switzerland, and Turkey. Within this group of countries, some ministries use a "light handed" approach to regulation that minimises *ex ante* regulation of the industry. In this approach, there is no specific industry regulation. However, the ministry retains a supervisory role, and the threat exists of introducing regulation if market performance is unsatisfactory. This approach has been explicitly adopted in New Zealand, where it is currently being reviewed, and is also present, to some extent, in Germany.

The basic approach to regulation adopted by each IEA member country is summarised in Table 2. Additional information on non-

Table 2

Institutional Approaches of IEA Countries to ESI Regulation: Role of Ministries and Regulatory Agencies

Country	General Approach (Main Institutions)	Observations
Australia	Ministry and independent regulatory agency	Both at federal and state Level
Austria	Ministry	
Belgium	Ministry and independent advisory and dispute resolution agency	
Canada	Ministry and independent regulatory agency	Both at federal and state Level
Czech Republic	Ministry	Ministerial agency planned for 2001
Denmark	Ministry and independent regulatory agency	
Finland	Ministry and independent regulatory agency	
France	Ministry and independent regulatory agency	
Germany	Ministry	Light-handed approach
Greece	Ministry and independent advisory and dispute resolution agency	
Hungary	Ministry and ministerial agency	
Ireland	Ministry and independent regulatory agency	
Japan	Ministry	
Luxembourg	Ministry and independent advisory and dispute resolution agency	
The Netherlands	Ministry and ministerial agency	
New Zealand	Ministry	Light handed approach
Norway	Ministry and ministerial agency	
Portugal	Ministry and independent regulatory agency	
Spain	Ministry and independent advisory and dispute resolution agency	
Sweden	Ministry and independent regulatory agency	
Switzerland	Ministry	Federal and cantonal Governments
Turkey	Ministry	
United Kingdom	Ministry and independent regulatory agency	
United States	Ministry and independent regulatory agency	Both at federal and state Level

ministerial regulatory agencies operating in IEA countries is provided in Table 3 and Figures 1 and 2.

■ Competition Law

Competition authorities have jurisdiction over the ESI in most IEA countries. However, competition authorities often have concurrent

Table 3

Independent Regulatory Agencies in the ESI

	Australia*	Canada*	Finland	Ireland	Italy
Scope	Energy, telecoms and airports	Electricity, gas and oil	Electricity	Electricity	Electricity and gas
Board Members	7	9	1	1 (could increase to 3)	3
Length of appoinment (Years)	Up to 5 years	7	Indefinite	Up to 7	7
Possibility of renewal	Yes	Yes	—	Yes (only once)	No
Staff (1999)	370 (of these, 11 deal with electricity	280	10	**	80
Budget (Million US$, 1997)	31.5	19	0.9	**	9.7
Main source of financing	Treasury's Budget	Annual fees paid by the regulated companies (based on volume of regulated activity)	Supervision and permit fees on network activities	** Paid by electricity undertakings (to be determined)	Tax on utilities revenue not to exceed 1 per thousand of regulated industry income
Main functions	Network regulation; wholesale market rules; antitrust	Regulation of electricity exports	Licensing of network activities; network price regulation (ex post)	Network regulation; Licensing	End user tariffs; network regulation

* *Federal regulatory agency.*
** *Data not yet available. The Office is currently being established.*

Table 3 Continued

	Portugal	Spain	Sweden	United Kingdom	United States*
Scope	Electricity telecoms	Electricity, gas and oil	Electricity	Electricity and gas	Electricity, gas and oil
Board Members	3	9	1	1	5
Length of appoinment (Years)	5	6	Indefinite	5	5
Possibility of renewal	Yes	Yes, one time	—	Yes, one time	Yes
Staff approx. (1999)	42	118	***	233 (Year 97)	1377 (Year 97) (ESI only: 470)
Budget approx. (Million US$, Year 1997)	3.1	6.5	***	21	154
Main source of financing	Surcharge on transmission tariffs	Surcharge on consumption not to exceed 0.5 per 1,000 of electricity revenue	***	Charge on the income of the regulated parties	Fees for services (filing fees) and annual charges on utilities
Main functions	End user tariffs	Approves Mergers and Acquisitions of transmission and distribution companies	Network price regulation (ex post)	End user tariffs; licensing	Rules for interstate electricity sales and transmission; transmission and wholesale tariffs; overseeing Mergers

* *Federal regulatory agency.*
*** *Integrated within the Swedish National Energy Administration which employs about 160 staff and has an annual turnover of about 1 Million SEK.*

jurisdiction with other entities, and co-ordination is needed. The most common approach is that the competition authority enforces competition law, including cases of abuse of dominant position, other anti-competitive behaviour and mergers, and the ministry and regulatory offices manage regulation. This is often complemented with some formal or informal co-operation arrangements to facilitate the exchange of information. There are, however, significant departures from this approach:

- In Australia, competition law and most regulatory issues are under the responsibility of the same independent agency. This applies both at the federal and state levels.
- In the Netherlands, competition law and regulation are also under the control of a single institution, namely the Ministry.
- In the US and the UK, merger policy is concurrently enforced by the energy regulatory agency and the antitrust enforcement office.

Box 1

A Summary of the EU Framework

EU Internal Electricity Market

The Council of the European Union adopted a directive on the internal market for electricity (EC 96/92) on 19 December 1996. EU Member States had, with some exceptions, implemented the directive into their national laws by 19 February 1999. Ireland and Belgium had one additional year and Greece has two additional years to comply with the Directive. France complied in February 2000.

Under the directive, increasing shares of electricity markets must be opened to competition. By 2000, the largest users accounting for 30% of consumption had the right to choose supplier. This percentage has to increase to 35% in 2003.

Access to the network is via a transmission services operator who must be separate (at least as a separate business unit) from generation and distribution businesses. EU member states can choose from three different procedures for access. Under regulated third-party access, tariffs for access to the networks are regulated, published and are available to all parties. Under negotiated third-party access, eligible consumers or generators/suppliers can negotiate network access with the incumbent utility. Prices and access terms are agreed freely among them and are confidential. The system operators must be involved in the negotiations and must publish an indicative range of transmission and distribution prices on an annual basis. The third possible approach is the "single-buyer" system, so-called because a designated single buyer sells all electricity to final consumers, but eligible consumers are free to conclude supply contracts with generators or suppliers both inside and outside the incumbent utility's territory.

There are two options for adding generating capacity. Under the "tendering" procedure, the monopoly utility determines when new capacity is required and conducts a tender for this requirement. Under the "authorisation" procedure, the timing of generating capacity investments is the responsibility of individual investors, provided they meet criteria specified in advance by the member state for the granting of an authorisation to construct. Member states may also opt not to require any particular procedure and leave the whole matter to market forces.

Member states may impose public service obligations to ensure "security, including security of supply, regularity, quality and price of supplies and ... environmental protection". The directive also permits member states to impose a requirement that up to 15% of fuels to be used in the generation of electricity come from indigenous sources.

Cross-border transactions are a major bottleneck in the development of the internal EU electricity market. The old pricing and capacity-allocation mechanisms for international transmission lines are grossly inadequate in the new framework. Cross-border tariffs often discourage trade and do not generally reflect the cost of transmission. Also, non-discriminatory access to the network is undermined by long-term contracts and agreements granting access to cross-border transmission capacity to certain companies and not others. The EU Commission has launched what is known as the Florence process to establish common rules for cross-border transmission within the EU that are consistent with the development of the internal market.

Source: IEA

Box 1 Continued

A Summary of the EU Framework

EU Competition Law

The European Union has has common legislation to protect competition since 1958. Agreements that distort competition and the abuse of a dominant position are both prohibited. The purpose of these provisions is to prevent agreements or abuses on the part of companies enjoying a dominant position from damaging trade between member states. The borderline between Community legislation and national legislation is not totally clear. Community law applies whenever effective competition in the Common Market or in a substantial part of it is significantly impeded.

Since 1990, there has been a merger control system. Before two or more undertakings may merge, they must notify the EU Commission of their intention. The Commission may prohibit the operation whenever it substantially impedes competition in the Common Market or in a substantial part of it. Acquisitions and mergers fall within the scope of the system when they have a "Community dimension", as determined by the size of the companies involved.

Responsibility for guaranteeing the enforcement of competition law at the Community level lies with the European Commission.

Source: EU Commission and Italian Competition Authority

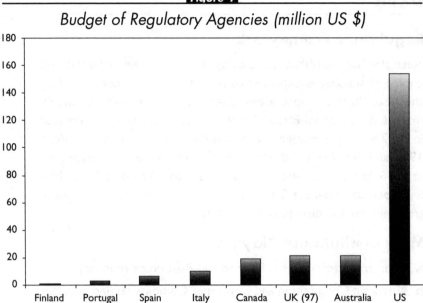

Figure 1

Budget of Regulatory Agencies (million US $)

Source: IEA (Table 3)

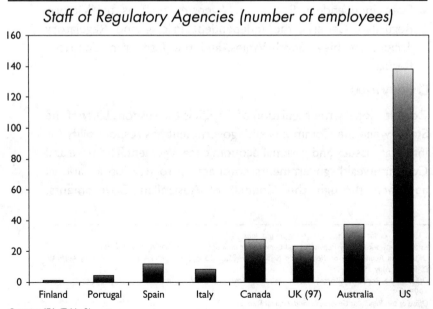

Figure 2

Staff of Regulatory Agencies (number of employees)

Source: IEA (Table 3)

Australia[13]

☐ Regulatory Framework

Australia has regulated third-party access to the network and choice of supplier is expected to be available to all consumers by the year 2001 in most areas. There is a mandatory wholesale market, the National Electricity Market of Australia. It was created in 1997 from the merger of the Victoria market, in operation since 1994, and the New South Wales market, established as a daily pool in 1996. Entry into generation is subject to a licensing procedure and open to all parties. There is vertical unbundling of generation, transmission and distribution activities.

☐ Main Institutional Players

- Department of Industry, Science and Resources (Ministry).
- Australian Competition and Consumer Commission (Independent Regulatory Agency and Competition Authority).
- State Governments.
- State Independent Regulatory Agencies such as the Victoria Regulator General, the Independent Pricing and Regulatory Tribunal of New South Wales, and the Tasmanian Electricity Regulator.

☐ Overview

Constitutionally, the regulation of the ESI is the responsibility of the States while the Commonwealth government has responsibility for interstate issues and national economic management. The state and Commonwealth governments co-operated to develop a national approach through the Council of Australian Governments.

---

13. ACCC: About ACCC. http://www.accc.gov.au/. June 1999.
Asher, A. Network Industry Regulation and Convergence in Supply Delivery. APPEA Journal, 1998.
OECD: Mini Round Table on Relationship between Regulators and Competition Authorities, Note by Australia. DAFFE. 27 May 1998.
Office of the Regulator General, Victoria: Objectives. Structure. Electricity. In http://www.reggen.vic.gov.au/. June 1999.
Office of the Regulator General, Victoria: Annual Report 97/98.
Some information directly provided to the IEA Secretariat by ACCC.

Following the adoption of a comprehensive plan in 1995 to create a competitive National Electricity Market (NEM), the institutional landscape has changed considerably. An independent national electricity regulator has been established – the Australian Competition and Consumer Commission (ACCC) – as well as number of independent state regulators; as an example, the Office of the Regulator-General of Victoria will be considered below.

Most regulatory functions are performed by the independent regulatory agencies with the national agency specialising in the regulation of transmission and wholesale markets and the state regulators specialising in distribution and retail. However, the federal government also has an important, albeit indirect, role in the development of regulation as some financial assistance programs to the states are linked to the satisfactory progress of reforms. The Ministry of Industry, Science and Resources also conducts policy in other energy areas such as energy efficiency, R&D, environmental protection and international energy issues. In the states examined the main role of the state governments in regulatory issues is to set the mandate of the state regulatory agencies.

Various organisations deal with the operation of the market. The National Electricity Code Administrator monitors compliance with rules of the National Electricity Market and raises Code breaches with the National Electricity Tribunal. In addition, a reliability panel determines power system security and reliability standards, and monitors market reliability.

The Australian system is unique in two key aspects. First, the national regulator, the ACCC, is also the competition authority. Second, the ACCC is a multi-sector regulator also covering gas, telecommunications and airports.

■ The Australian Competition and Consumer Commission (ACCC)

The ACCC was formed on 6 November 1995 by the merger of the Trade Practices Commission and the Prices Surveillance Authority.

It is the body responsible for administering and enforcing the Trade Practices Act that applies to all sectors, including electricity. This law deals with anti-competitive and unfair market practices, including misuse of market power, secondary boycotts and anti-competitive mergers. The ACCC provides for the surveillance and monitoring of prices in certain industries and has general cross-sector responsibilities. It advises the government on rights of access to essential infrastructures and, where these rights have been established, acts as "arbitrator of last resort", determining access conditions and prices in case of disputes. Finally, the ACCC also has a significant role in promoting competition through regulatory reform in Australia.

In addition, the ACCC has specific regulatory responsibilities regarding the ESI. These are:

Regulation of the Network:

- Developing accounting and reporting rules and benchmarks for electricity transmission and advising state regulators on similar rules for distribution companies.
- Setting service standards for transmission network performance.
- Determining the annual revenue requirement for each transmission company operating in the national electricity market for a five year period.
- Developing the details of regulatory policy such as the different forms of incentive regulation that may be applied.
- Approval of interconnector proposals and capital expenditures.
- Approval of access arrangements to the network.

Organisation of the Market:

- Evaluation and approval of changes to the "Code" that governs the operation of the market.
- Development of future market arrangements such as the future structure of network charges, market design and retail competition.

Promotion and Defence of Competition:

- Investigation of market arrangements and behaviour that may contravene the antitrust laws.

- Evaluation of electricity industry mergers.

The Commission comprises a chairperson, a deputy chairperson and five commissioners. They are appointed by the Federal government after consultation with the states for an irrevocable term of up to five years and are eligible for re-appointment. There is some 370 staff. A total of eleven staff members work in the electricity regulation team. In addition, competition law issues in the electricity sector, such as mergers, involve other teams. Out of a total budget of the order of A$ 50 million, the amount allocated to electricity work, including externally procured consulting services but not including overhead, was about A$ 1.5 million in 2000. This is financed mainly with appropriations from the Treasury's budget plus a smaller amount obtained from authorisation fees and fines.

■ The Office of the Regulator General, Victoria

In operation since 1994, the Office regulates electricity, water, gas, grain handling and ports within the state of Victoria. The general objectives of the Office are to promote competition, to defend competition and to ensure that consumers benefit from competition. In addition, the Office manages a number of specific measures defined in the relevant sectoral acts.

The functions of the Office related to electricity concern mainly distribution and retail supply. These are:

Regulation of the Network:

- Setting price controls for distribution and approval of distribution tariffs.

- Approval of transmission and other charges applying in the Victoria Power Exchange.

- Setting service standards for distribution and other related services and monitoring compliance.

Regulation of Retailing:

- Approval of retail tariffs for franchised consumers.
- Setting service standards for retail services and monitoring compliance.
- Development of retailer of last resort scheme.

Promotion and Defence of Competition:

- Monitoring market conduct of retailers and distributors.
- Information programs to customers.
- Introduction of competition in other supply related services, such as metering.

Licensing:

- Issuing licences for all electricity companies – generators, retailers and network service providers – operating in the state. Licences are granted on the basis of financial and technical criteria.

The Office comprises one member appointed as the Regulator-General for a five year period. It employs a staff of about 33 members and had an annual operating budget of the order of A$ 6.8 million in 1998, financed mainly by the State. The administrative structure of the Office reflects functions rather than sectors and therefore no breakdown for electricity is available.

■ Co-ordination Between Federal and State Authorities

There is potential for some overlap of functions between the ACCC and the state regulators. A number of steps have been taken to minimise uncertainty regarding jurisdiction and to avoid confusion. The ACCC has frequent information exchanges with state regulators through regular liaison meetings and the exchange of publications and other information. In addition, chairpersons of various Commonwealth and State economic regulators such as the Victorian Office of the Regulator General are associate members of the ACCC. These measures are intended to bridge the "knowledge gap" that can arise between the separate bodies.

Austria[14]

□ Regulatory Framework

Third-party access to the network is regulated and a gradual opening of the market is planned; currently all customers with more than 40 GWh yearly consumption and distribution companies that also operate a transmission system can choose their supplier. Entry into generation activities is governed by an authorisation system and open to all parties. There is unbundling of accounts for transmission activities as required in the EU electricity directive.

□ Main Institutional Players

- Ministry of Economic Affairs.
- Competition Authority (Kartellgericht).

□ Overview

At federal level, the main regulatory authority is the Ministry of Economic Affairs. The ministry is responsible for developing legislation and general energy policy, and making decisions on energy and energy supply networks.

The specific functions of the Ministry in electricity include:

- Determining all regulated access and electricity tariffs.
- Acting as the arbitrator for refusals of access cases.

---

14. EU DG XVII: Implementation of the EU Directive by Member states.
http://europa.eu.int/en/comm/dg17/elechome.htm. September 1999.
IEA: Energy Policies of IEA Countries, Austria 1998 Review. 1998.

Additionally, there is a consultative committee (Elektrizitätsbeirat) in which various social parties are represented. This committee proposes tariff structures and calculation principles and serves as a consultative body to the Ministry on all new electricity regulation.

The authorities of the Länder have an important role in the energy sector. They are responsible for the authorisation of new generation capacity, are in charge of legal instruments for energy conservation, such as building codes, and provide subsidies for energy conservation measures and for renewables.

■ Competition

Competition law applies to the ESI. Cases concerning abuse of dominant position and other aspects of competition law have to be referred to the Competition Authority (Kartellgericht).

Belgium[15]

□ Regulatory Framework

Belgium has regulated third-party access to the network. However, a system of negotiated access is planned for cross-border electricity transit and the transmission of large quantities. There will be a gradual opening of the market; currently, consumers with more than 20 GWh yearly consumption can choose their supplier; the eligibility threshold will be reduced to 10 GWh not later than the end of 2002, and by 2007 all consumers directly connected to the transmission network will be eligible. Entry into generation is subject to an authorisation procedure. The Transmission System Operator is a separate company and is not allowed to have interests in other electricity companies or to perform other activities than the operation, maintenance and development of the

15. Electrabel: Annual Report 1998.
EU DG XVII: Implementation of the EU Directive by member states.
http://europa.eu.int/en/comm/dg17/elechome.htm. September 1999.
Belgium: Loi du 5 août 1991 sur la protection de la concurrence économique.

network. In addition, there is unbundling of accounts for electric activities as required by the EU Directive.

☐ Main Regulatory Authorities

- Ministry of Economic Affairs.
- The Electricity and Gas Regulation Commission.
- Regional governments and regulation bodies of Flanders, Wallonia and Brussels.
- The Competition Authority (Conseil de la Concurrence).

☐ Overview

The Ministry of Economic Affairs has ultimate responsibility for most regulatory activities concerning the electricity industry with the exception of the distribution function which, to a large extent, falls within the jurisdiction of the regional governments. In addition to taxation and developing general legislation, the functions of the Ministry include:

- Setting maximum national tariffs for non-eligible consumers.
- Approving tariffs and access conditions for transmission.
- Approving national requirements for generating and transmission capacity.
- Nuclear issues.

There is an independent advisory body to the Ministry, the Electricity and Gas Regulatory Commission, composed of a chairperson and five other members appointed for a renewable period of six years by the Council of Ministers. The functions of the Commission are:

- Advising government in the drafting of laws and regulations concerning the electricity market.
- Supervising and monitoring their application.
- Running a conciliation and arbitration service for any disputes in connection with access to the transmission network. An administrative appeals tribunal can review the Commission's decisions in this area.

The Commission is assisted by a General Advisory Council composed of Federal and Regional Government representatives and representatives of the industry's social and economic interests. Its operating costs are financed with a charge on transmission tariffs.

■ Competition

Competition law applies, in principle, to the electricity industry. The competition authority is the Conseil de la Concurrence, an administrative judicial body linked to the Ministry of Economic Affairs. It works in collaboration with the Electricity and Gas Regulatory Commission, which has conciliation and arbitration powers.

Canada[16]

□ Regulatory Framework

There is a federal system with significant differences among the provinces. Only Alberta and Ontario have firm plans to give all consumers a choice of supplier, both in the next 12 months. Both provinces have regulated third-party access to the network and transmission is operated by separate entities. Alberta has set up a mandatory competitive spot market and a voluntary spot market is planned to start operation in Ontario this year.

□ Main Institutional Players

- Ministry of Natural Resources.
- National Energy Board.
- Provincial energy ministries such as the Ontario Ministry of Energy, Science and Technology and the Alberta Resources Development Department.

16. Alberta Resource Development web page http://www.energy.gov.ab.ca/. January 2000.
Canada Competition Bureau web site. http://strategis.ic.gc.ca/SSG/ct01254e.html. January 2000.
National Energy Board: Home, NEB web site. http://www.neb.gc.ca/. October 1999.
OECD: Application of Competition Policy to the Electricity Sector. OECD/GD(97)132. 1997.
Ontario Energy Board: Home, OEB web site. http://www.oeb.gov.on.ca/. October 1999.
Ontario Ministry of Energy, Science and Technology: web site http://www.est.gov.on.ca/english/index.html. January 2000.

- Provincial Regulators, such as the Ontario Energy Board and the Alberta Energy and Utilities Board.
- The Federal Competition Bureau.

□ Overview

The Ministry of Natural Resources has overall responsibility for federal energy policy, international energy issues, environmental issues pertaining to energy, sustainable development and other long-term strategies, fiscal analysis, forecasting and other cross-cutting energy issues.

In addition, there is a national regulator, the National Energy Board (NEB), that has jurisdiction over decisions relating to exports of electricity and to the construction and operation of international and some inter-provincial power lines.

Responsibility for the electricity industry is principally held at the provincial government level. Provincial ministries have a key role in promoting and developing the new regulatory frameworks that are being proposed for the electricity supply industry. For example, the Ontario Ministry of Energy is implementing the Energy Competition Act, 1998. This includes setting guidelines for the opening of the market, market rules, licencing and consumer protection.

Each of the provinces also has an independent regulatory agency that develops and applies regulation within the framework set by the Ministry. These are multi-sector, independent and quasi-judicial regulatory agencies covering all forms of energy. As an example, the Ontario Energy Board (OEB) is considered below.

The co-ordination of provincial regulations to promote inter-provincial trade has been the subject of discussion and interest by the provincial governments. Discussions between the provinces and the federal government on this matter are continuing.

■ The National Energy Board (NEB)

NEB is an independent federal regulatory agency that was established in 1959. The Board regulates the gas, oil and electricity sectors, provides advice to the federal government and conducts studies on the energy sector. Concerning electricity, NEB authorizes the construction and operation of international power lines and designated inter-provincial lines under federal jurisdiction, and issues export permits. NEB does not regulate electricity imports.

The Board is accountable to Parliament, to which it reports, through the Minister of Natural Resources.

The Board operates in a very similar way to a court. Its powers include the swearing in and examination of witnesses and the taking of evidence. Under the NEB Act, up to nine Board Members may be appointed. Appointments are for a seven-year term and are renewable. Approximately 280 employees assist NEB members. Expenses for 1998 were in the order of C$ 28 million. These are financed through annual fees charged on the regulated companies. Charges are calculated on the basis of the volume of the regulated activity that each company performs.

■ The Ontario Energy Board (OEB)

OEB is an independent, quasi-judicial tribunal created by the Ontario Energy Board Act of 1998. It operates independently from the Ministry and all other government departments. The Board has regulatory oversight of both natural gas and electricity matters in the province and also provides advice on energy matters referred to it by the provincial Minister of Energy, Science and Technology and the provincial Minister of Natural Resources. Reforms in the electricity sector have been enacted and will come into effect in the year 2001.

In the electricity sector the functions of the OEB are:

Regulation of the Network:

- Approving transmission and distribution rates.
- Approving distribution and transmission line construction.
- Approving mergers and acquisitions such as distributor amalgamations, acquisitions of an interest in a generator by a

transmitter or distributor or their affiliates, acquisition of an interest in a distributor or transmitter by a generator or its affiliate, and the sale, lease or disposition by a transmitter or distributor of a transmission or distribution system.

Regulation of Wholesale Energy Prices:

■ Approving Ontario Hydro Services Company Inc. (OHSC) rates.

Promotion and Defence of Competition:

■ Monitoring markets in the electricity sector and reporting to the Minister on the efficiency, fairness, transparency and competitiveness of the markets.

■ Reporting on any abuse or potential abuse of market power.

Licensing:

■ Licensing all participants including the Independent Market Operator (IMO), generators, transmitters, distributors, wholesalers and retailers.

The OEB comprises ten members, including a chairperson, assisted by approximately 45 staff members. All costs incurred are recovered from the business organisations subject to licensing or regulation by the OEB. OEB costs are recovered from the licence holders through fixed annual fees and application fees set by the Ministry of Energy of the Province. The structure of OEB's fees is currently under review.

■ Competition

Canadian Competition Law applies to the electricity sector but only on those aspects regulated at the Federal level. Thus, the Competition Bureau does not have jurisdiction on those aspects of ESI activity that are regulated at the provincial level. The provincial governments and regulators have jurisdiction on these aspects. However, in Alberta, it has been decided that the Electricity Market Surveillance Authority will refer any cases of suspected anticompetitive business behaviour directly to the Competition Bureau for investigation and possible action. In addition, the Bureau has been active in promoting regulatory reform in the Canadian electricity sector.

Czech Republic[17]

☐ Regulatory Framework

There is a state-owned generation and transmission company (CEZ), eight distribution companies and a number of independent power producers which are connected to the distribution networks. Distribution companies can buy energy from CEZ and from the independent power producers. Currently, there is no third-party access to the transmission network and no market opening. However, in the context of adapting regulation to the EU directive, it is planned that there will be regulated third-party access in the future. Transmission is carried out by a separate company owned by CEZ.

☐ Main Institutional Players

- The Ministry of Industry and Trade (MIT).
- The Energy Regulation Administration, currently a Department of MIT, that will become an autonomous ministerial agency in 2001.
- The Ministry of Finance.

☐ Overview

The Ministry of Industry and Trade (MIT) has overall responsibility for energy policy, Including general policy objectives, development of the energy sector, industry supervision and climate change. The Ministry of Finance (MOF) is responsible for tariffs, ownership and competition. The Ministry of Environment (MOE) portfolio includes emissions regulation and control, climate change, and certain issues related to nuclear and energy policies.

---

17. *Czech Republic: Submission to the IEA for the Review of Czech Energy Policies (2000).*

The Energy Regulatory Administration (ERA) was created as a Department of MIT in 1998. It is planned that it will take over responsibility for the licensing of operators, structure and levels of tariffs, system operation and monitoring of competition. It is also planned that ERA will operate as an autonomous state administration with a state budget allocation.

■ Competition

The Office for the Protection of Economic Competition within the Ministry of Finance is the anti monopoly body. It has jurisdiction over the ESI.

Denmark[18]

□ Regulatory Framework

The Danish electricity industry is now embarked on the transition to a competitive market. There is regulated third-party access to the network and market opening is being introduced rapidly, with all consumers having choice of supplier by 2003. Entry into generation is subject to an authorisation procedure that takes into account planning requirements. In addition to the unbundling of accounts required by the EU Directive, the different functions have to be performed by separate legal entities.

□ Main Institutional Players

- The Ministry of Environment and Energy.
- The Energy Supervisory Board, an independent regulatory body that substitutes the Electricity Price Committee.
- The Danish Competition Council assisted by the Competition Authority.

---

18. *Denmark: Competition Act. 1997.*
Denmark: Energy Supply Act. 1999.
IEA: Regulatory Reform in Denmark (Electricity). Draft. January 2000.
OECD: Mini Round Table on Relationship between Regulators and Competition Authorities, Note by Denmark. DAFFE. 27 May 1998.

☐ Overview

Plans to reform the ESI were approved in 1999 and came into force in 2000. According to the new Energy Act, regulatory functions are shared between a ministerial agency and an independent body that administers regulated electricity prices.

The Danish Energy Agency (DEA), an agency within the Ministry of Environment and Energy, is responsible for energy policy formulation and implementation. In particular, the DEA performs the following functions:

- Overall planning of power, heat, and natural gas.
- Licensing of all electricity industry activities.
- Implementation of environmental policies that apply to the sector.

A new inspection authority – the Energy Supervisory Board – was created in 1999 to replace the Electricity Price Committee and the Gas and Heat Price Committee. The main roles of the Board are:

- Supervising end user prices and delivery conditions and amending them whenever they are found to be unreasonable or to result in an environmentally or economically inappropriate use of energy.
- Setting tariffs for transmission under a general framework established by the Ministry.

The Board is an independent agency consisting of a Chairman and six other members appointed by the Minister for Environment and Energy for a period of four years, and it is endowed with powers to request information and to enforce sanctions for non-compliance. The staff of the Board will consist of officials of both the Danish Energy Agency and the Competition Authority.

■ Competition

The Danish Competition Act applies to the electricity sector provided that it is not in conflict with the Energy Supply Act. The secretariat of the Competition Council is the competition authority (Konkurrencestyrelsen). The Authority also performs secretariat services for the for the Energy Supervisory Board.

Finland[19]

☐ Regulatory Framework

There has been regulated third-party access to the network since 1995. All consumers may choose their supplier. Electricity is traded both bilaterally and through the Nordic Power Exchange (NordPool). There is an authorisation procedure for entry into generation that is not subject to any energy specific criteria. Transmission is owned and operated by a separate company, which is partly owned by the state, power producers and other institutional investors, so that no one has a dominant position in the firm. There is unbundling of accounts for generation, distribution and sale activities.

☐ Main Institutional Players

- The Ministry of Trade and Industry.
- The Electricity Market Authority, the independent regulatory agency.
- The Finnish Competition Authority.

☐ Overview

Regulatory activities are split between the Ministry of Trade and Industry and an independent regulatory agency, the Electricity Market Authority (Sähkömarkkinakeskus or SMK). The role of the Ministry of Trade and Industry is to develop new legislation such as

---

19. *Finland: Electricity Market Act. 386/95.*
IEA: Energy Policies of Finland, 1999 Review.
EU DG XVII: Implementation of the EU Directive by member states.
http://europa.eu.int/en/comm/dg17/elechome.htm. September 1999.
OECD: Mini Round Table on Relationship between Regulators and Competition Authorities, Note by Finland. DAFFE. 27 May 1998.
SMK: Annual Report. 1998.
Some information directly provided to the Secretariat by the Ministry of Trade and Industry.

bills subject to parliamentary approval, decrees and ministerial decisions. The Ministry is also responsible for issuing licences for the construction of high voltage transborder lines.

The Electricity Market Act (1995) provided for the establishment of the SMK with a particular responsibility to supervise compliance with the Act. SMK main function is the monitoring of network activities. It must be noted that transmission tariffs are monitored but not set by SMK since, in Finland, there is no ongoing transmission price regulation. In particular, SMK activities include:

Regulation of the Network:

- Monitoring general obligations of transmission and distribution service providers including the development and maintenance of their systems, obligations to give access, provide other services and publish information, and to assess if they are equitable and non-discriminatory.

- Monitoring pricing principles of network operation to assess if they are equitable and non-discriminatory.

Retailing:

- Monitoring end-user prices and the electricity retailer's obligation to deliver electricity.

Licensing:

- Issuing licences for network operation.
- Issuing licences for construction of national high voltage lines of 110 kV or above.

Dispute Resolution:

- Acting as the first instance arbitrator in case of disputes.

In addition, SMK serves in an advisory role to other authorities, companies and consumers in matters relating to the Electricity Act and compiles information as required to monitor network and retailing activities.

SMK makes its rulings based on the Electricity Market Act, independently from the Ministry of Trade and Industry, and is the only body that officially interprets the Act. SMK decisions can be appealed to the Supreme Administrative Court of Justice. The Government appoints the Head of SMK for an indefinite mandate.

As of 1999, SMK had 10 professional staff and a budget of the order of 5.5 million Finnish K. Most of the budget, around 90%, is financed from supervision and permit fees, which are charged on the network business. The rest comes from the state budget.

■ Competition

The Finnish competition authority (Kilpailuvirasto or OFC) may fully apply the Act on Competition Restrictions to electricity production and distribution. SMK and the OFC have concurrent jurisdiction concerning pricing decisions taken by producers and distributors of electricity, and pricing policies by dominant transmission companies and dominant retail sellers of electricity. Each of the two authorities informs the other of newly opened files, consults the other concerning pending cases, and customarily reserves the other an opportunity to make a written comment on its draft decisions. Thus, there is an informal but stable agreement between the two authorities concerning their division of labour. In addition the OFC is obliged to ask for a statement from the SMK in merger cases related to the electricity sector.

France[20]

□ Regulatory Framework

France has adopted a model of regulated third-party access to the network and the largest consumers can choose supplier in line with the minimum market opening levels prescribed in the EU

---

20. EU DG XVII: Implementation of the EU Directive by member states.
http://europa.eu.int/en/comm/dg17/elechome.htm. September 1999.
Ministere de l'Economie Web page. http://www.industrie.gouv.fr/cgi-bin/industrie/frame0.pl?url=/energie/.
January 2000.
Jenny, Frederic: "Regulateurs Sectoriels et Autorites de Concurrence en France et en Europe". Mimeo. 18 Mai 1999.

directive. Entry into generation can be subject either to tendering or to an authorisation procedure in accordance with criteria that still have to be specified. There is unbundling of accounts as required by the directive and, in addition, system operation will be independently managed.

☐ Main Institutional Players

- Ministry of Economics, Finance and Industry.
- Electricity Regulation Commission, an independent regulatory agency.
- The Competition Authority (Conseil de la Concurrence).

☐ Overview

The Ministry of Economics, Finance and Industry is responsible for most aspects of regulation and energy policy with the exception of the regulation of the network. Ministry responsibilities include public service obligations, general technical regulations for the electricity sector and safeguarding the security and smooth operation of the system. It also supervises the industry to ensure that these objectives are met.

Public service obligations include the supply of electricity, the development and operation of the networks as a universal service in order to guarantee of supply to all consumers throughout the country, geographical equalisation of tariffs and assistance for hardship cases. Other priorities of French energy policy are long-term security of supply and the competitiveness of the economy.

Responsibility for network access issues was transferred from the Ministry to an independent agency in March 2000. In step with the transposition of the EU directive into national legislation, the independent Electricity Regulation Commission was established with responsibility to:

- Ensure fair and transparent transmission tariffs and access to the electricity network.
- Arbitrate disputes concerning network access.

- Advise to the Ministry in other areas of regulation, including tariffs for end users.

The Commission has the power to impose penalties for non-compliance by the industry with their obligations.

The Commission comprises six members, three appointed by the executive and the other three by the Presidents of the National Assembly, the Senate and the Economic and Social Council. Appointments are for a non-renewable six year period. It employed a staff of about 55 by the end of the year 2000. It is financed with funds appropriated from the state budget.

While initially the Commission has responsibility for electricity only, its coverage is likely to extend to the regulation of gas in the future.

■ Competition

Competition law applies to the ESI except when in conflict with the specific regulation of the industry, including public service obligations. The competition authority is the "Conseil de la Concurrence".

Germany[21]

☐ Regulatory Framework

Germany has negotiated third-party access to the network with a parallel Single Buyer option for distribution companies until 2005. All consumers can choose their supplier. Entry into generation is not subject to any specific procedure. The industry is vertically integrated and there is unbundling of accounts, as required in the EU Directive. However, some electricity generators have

21. EU DG XVII: Implementation of the EU Directive by member states.
http://europa.eu.int/en/comm/dg17/elechome.htm. September 1999.
IEA: Energy Policies of Germany, 1998 Review.
Ministry of Economics (Germany) Web page. http://www.bmwi.de/. February 2000.
OECD: Mini Round Table on Relationship between Regulators and Competition Authorities, Note by Germany. DAFFE. 27 May 1998.

transferred their transmission network to a legally separated entity.

☐ Main Institutional Players

- The Federal Ministry of Economy.
- The Governments of the Laender.
- The Federal Competition Authority.

☐ Overview

The Ministry of Economy is responsible for energy policy and has general authority over the ESI. The Ministry is responsible, in particular, for international activities, analysis of the energy market, rational energy use, renewables, energy research (in particular as it relates to new energy transformation techniques and renewable energies) phase-out of nuclear, environmental and climate protection statutes, overseeing the ESI and district heating.

The German approach to electricity regulation is based on applying the same general regulations that apply to other industries. There is no ongoing price or access regulation for electricity except for small consumers. In this context, no specific electricity regulator exists.

The Laender governments are responsible for implementing Federal law. They are responsible for granting licences in their jurisdiction and, in particular, for the approval of new generating capacity, and applying general standards on land use, security and environmental protection. The Laender may take their own measures in the field of energy policy, including the promotion of renewables and energy efficiency.

■ Competition

The competition authorities – Landeskartellbehörden in the Laenders and the Bundeskartellamt at the federal level – are responsible for the application of competition law, notably regarding cases of abuse of dominant position, and dispute settlement concerning network access. The Federal Cartel Office has jurisdiction in all cases which have effects beyond the territory of a single Land, while the Laender Cartel Offices have jurisdiction on cases within their areas. The Federal Cartel Office decisions can be appealed to a tribunal, the Oberlandesgeritcht Dusseldorf, and then to the Federal Supreme Court.

The negotiated approach to network access means that litigation cases brought to the Bundeskartellamt have a significant role in creating precedent for many specific access issues. In addition, the institutional framework is complemented by voluntary industry agreements that aim to establish homogeneous criteria on pricing and other issues.

Greece[22]

☐ Regulatory Framework

Implementation of the EU Directive is effective from February 2001. There is negotiated third-party access to the network and limited consumer choice of supplier covering consumers of 100 GWh of annual consumption and higher. Entry into generation is subject to an authorisation procedure that may include specific energy criteria. It is planned that the industry will remain vertically integrated. There will be unbundling of accounts, as required in the EU Directive, and system operation will be managed by a legally separated entity.

☐ Main Institutional Players

- Ministry of Development.
- Energy Regulatory Authority.
- Competition Council.

---

22. *EU DG XVII: Implementation of the EU Directive by member states.* http://europa.eu.int/en/comm/dg17/elechome.htm. *September 1999.*
IEA: Energy policies of Greece. 1998.

□ Overview

All regulatory responsibilities are with the Ministry of Development. Control of the monopoly utility is exercised through power of appointment to the Board of Directors and top management of the utility. The Ministry of Development is responsible for coordinating the development plans of the company with state energy policy and for approving electricity tariffs. The Ministry of National Economy approves the company's financing programmes.

An independent Energy Regulatory Authority serve as a consultative body on electricity, natural gas and other energy sector matters. Its specific tasks are to:

■ Advise the Ministry on the granting of licenses.

■ Monitor the electricity market and collect information.

■ Impose fines for non-compliance.

■ Make proposals for the adoption of new measures and regulations.

The Authority has administrative and economic autonomy and the Ministry of Development will appoint its members and monitor its activities.

■ Competition

The Greek Competition Act applies, in principle, to the ESI. However, the government can exempt public undertakings such as the electricity state-owned company from competition law. The competition authority is the Competition Council.

Hungary[23]

□ Regulatory Framework

The Hungarian ESI is not yet open to competition. Generators are required to sell power to the state-owned incumbent monopoly

---

23. IEA: Energy Policies of Hungary. 1999 Review.
IEA: OECD Regulatory Reform Reviews: Hungary (Electricity Chapter). 1999.
OECD: Application of Competition Policy to the Electricity Sector. OCDE/GD(97)132. 1997.

power supplier (MVM) under long-term contracts, and distributors are required to buy it from MVM under long-term contracts. Prices and new investments in generation and transmission are regulated.

☐ Main Institutional Players

- Ministry of Economic Affairs.
- Hungarian Energy Office.
- Office of Economic Competition.

☐ Overview

The Minister of Economic Affairs is responsible for the regulation of the industry. It is assisted by the Hungarian Energy Office (Magyar Energia Hivatal, MEH) which is a form of a ministerial agency. The Ministry determines end-user prices and has authority on issues related to the construction of new power plants. However, for some large plants, these decisions are made by Parliament. The Minister can also influence the structure of the industry and major capital transactions under rights conferred by the "golden shares" the Government holds in power companies.

The ministerial agency, MEH, was established in 1994. It covers both electricity and natural gas. MEH conducts a number of advisory and support activities and also has some operational responsibilities. In particular, MEH is responsible for:

- Licensing and issuing construction permits for generation and transmission.
- Applying individual charges based on average pricing decisions and providing data for pricing decisions by the Ministry.
- Supervising the operations of license holders and monitoring of the market.
- Customer protection and, in particular, dealing with customer complaints.
- Approving of the terms of contracts involving regulated parties and mediating disputes between market participants.

- Monitoring and enforcing the network code, the dispatch code and the distribution code.

Government, through the Minister of Economic Affairs, supervises MEH. The Minister appoints the president, the vice presidents, and the director of administration for an indefinite term of office. Decisions made by the MEH can be appealed before the Courts. The Hungarian Energy office has 85 staff.

■ Competition

Actions based on orders by the Hungarian Energy Authorities are exempted from competition law. Thus, the Office of Economic Competition does not proceed in cases of abuse of dominant position when the complaint relates to electricity pricing policy in electricity cases, but forward these cases to the MEH. Both the MEH and the Office of Economic Competition must approve major mergers and acquisitions. This is the case for spin-offs, mergers involving license holders, if the merger results in a dominant position, reduction of capital by 25% or more, and acquisition of ownership stakes of 25% or more in electricity companies.

Ireland[24]

□ Regulatory Framework

The gradual opening of the Irish electricity market began in February 2000. It is based on regulated third-party access to the network and a choice of supplier for the largest consumers in line with the minimum requirements of the EU Directive covering those whose consumption is greater than 4 GWh. Entry into generation is subject to an authorisation procedure. There is a vertically integrated incumbent supplier, the Electricity Supply

---

24. EU DG XVII: Implementation of the EU Directive by member states.
http://europa.eu.int/en/comm/dg17/elechome.htm. September 1999.
IEA: Energy Policies of Ireland, 1999 Review.
Ireland: Electricity Regulation Act, 1999.
Ireland: Electricity Regulation Act, 1999, Criteria for Determination of Authorisations Order, 1999.

Board (ESB) that owns and operates the transmission and distribution networks. Provisions to implement the unbundling requirements of the EU Directive have not yet been introduced.

☐ Main Institutional Players

- Department of Public Enterprise.
- Commission for Electricity Regulation.
- Irish Competition Authority.

☐ Overview

The regulation of electricity is undertaken by the Ministry – Department of Public Enterprise – and an independent regulatory agency, established by the 1998 Electricity Bill, called the Commission for Electricity Regulation.

The Ministry is in charge of implementing energy policy and developing the general regulatory framework. In particular, it is responsible for:

- Setting end user tariffs.
- Approving the authorised revenue of the Electricity Supply Board, the publicly owned incumbent electricity supplier.

The Commission for Electricity Regulation main tasks are related to regulation of the network, issuing licences and dispute resolution. The main powers of the Commission are:

Regulation of the Network:

- Approving charges for connection and use of the system.
- Setting regulations on standards of performance.
- Requiring information and carrying out investigations on issues related to network activities.

Retailing:

- Regulating the amounts which may be recovered by ESB in respect of public service obligations.

Licensing:

◻ Granting licences authorising the generation and supply of electricity.

■ Modifying and revoking licences authorising the generation and supply of electricity.

■ Making and enforcing directions to ensure compliance with licences.

Dispute Resolution:

■ Settling disputes concerning access to the transmission and distribution system.

The Commission initially consists of one member but may be expanded to three members. Appointments are made for up to seven years and can be renewed once. The Commission's decisions are subject to an independent mechanism for appeals. It reports to a Joint Committee of the Oireachtas (parliament) and submits an annual report to the Minister for Public Enterprise. The Commission is funded through fees imposed on electricity undertakings.

■ Competition

The Competition Act of 1996 applies to the electricity sector. Breaches of competition law can be investigated by the Irish Competition Authority and, where necessary, it can bring civil and criminal court actions in order to stop anti-competitive arrangements or abuses of dominant positions.

Italy[25]

◻ Regulatory Framework

The market is organised around a regulated third-party access system that allows consumers with a minimum annual consumption

25. AEEG: Relazione Annuale sullo Stato dei Servizi E Sull'attivita Svolta. 1998 and 1999 Reports.
EU DG XVII: Implementation of the EU Directive by member states.
http://europa.eu.int/en/comm/dg17/elechome.htm. September 1999.
IEA: Energy Policies of Italy. 1999 Review.
OECD: Mini Round Table on Relationship between Regulators and Competition Authorities, Note by Italy.
DAFFE. 27 May 1998.

of 30 GWh to choose their supplier. Consumers with at least 2 GWh of annual consumption can enter consortia with neighboring consumers to reach the 30 GWh threshold. The eligibility limit will be reduced to 9 GWh by 2002. Entry into the generation business has been liberalised. Construction of new power plants is subject to environmental and local authorisations only. The different activities performed by the incumbent supplier (ENEL) will be performed by separate legal entities. The new companies will remain under ENEL's ownership except for system operation, which will be fully unbundled into a new company and owned by the Ministry of the Treasury.

☐ Main Institutional Players

- Ministry of Industry.
- Autorita per l'Energia Elettrica e il Gas (AEEG), an independent agency.
- Autorita garante della concorrenza e del mercato, the competition authority.
- Ministry of the Treasury.

☐ Overview

At the national level, the Ministry of Industry, the Ministry of the Treasury and the independent regulatory agency regulate the industry.

The Ministry of Industry conducts general energy policy. It is specifically responsible for licensing electricity companies and issuing building permits, and for setting technical standards for generation and distribution. Some policy tasks related to energy efficiency and the promotion of renewables are being progressively transferred to the regional authorities.

The Treasury, as owner of a majority stake in ENEL, has an influence on the restructuring and gradual privatisation of the industry. It will also remain owner of the new System Operator.

The independent regulatory agency for electricity and gas is the Autorità per l'Energia Elettrica e il Gas (AEEG). It was established in 1995 and has substantial regulatory powers. These powers have been extended following the March 1999 Decree that reformed the Italian ESI in compliance with the EU Directive.

AEEG is entrusted with an array of functions including the regulation of the network, consumer protection, end user tariffs, implementing unbundling obligations and some consultative and support activities. In particular, it is responsible for:

Regulation of the Network:

- Setting tariffs and conditions for third-party access to the network and for system operation.

Regulation of Retail Sales:

- Setting maximum tariffs for electricity according to a price cap formula.

Organisation of the Market:

- Setting directives for accounting methodology and unbundling.
- Establishing and enforcing quality standards for services and penalties for non-compliance.

Licensing:

- Making proposals to the Ministry of Industry on renewals, modification and suppression of concessions.

Other:

- Advising the government and the parliament on issues related to electricity.
- Dealing with customers complaints.

To carry out these tasks, AEEG has powers to request information from the regulated parties, to inspect them and to fine them for non-compliance.

The authority is an independent collegial body composed of a president and two members, appointed by the Italian president, after approval by parliament. Members are appointed for a nonrevocable seven year mandate, are not allowed to have other professional activities or direct economic interests in the regulated sector. They cannot be re-appointed. Its decisions are subject to appeal to an administrative court, then to the Council of State. The government can issue general guidelines that the authority is not obliged to follow.

In 1999, it had 80 staff. It is financed through a tax on the revenue of utilities that cannot exceed 1 per 1,000 of the regulated industry income. Expenditure for 1998 amounted to nearly 19,000 million lire.

■ Competition

The general approach governing the interaction between regulators and competition authorities has been to allocate the enforcement of competition policy in all sectors to the general competition authority (Autorità garante della concorrenza e del mercato) and regulatory tasks to sectorial regulatory bodies. More specifically, the Competition Act, fully applies to all economic sectors and the competition authority is responsible for enforcing it on an exclusive basis. However, AEEG monitors the ESI and reports any suspected violations of competition law to the competition authority.

Japan[26]

□ Regulatory Framework

The Government adopted in 1998 a program of partial liberalisation of its ESI. This was implemented in March 2000 and is to be reviewed three years later. There will be negotiated third-party access to the network. Large customers who use more than 2 MW and take power at 20,000 volts or above will be eligible to choose their supplier. They account for about 30% of total

---

26. IEA: OECD Regulatory Reform Project: Electricity Chapter of Japan (1998).
IEA: Energy Policies of Japan. 1999 Review.

electricity demand. Other related measures include a re-examination of the electricity rate system, the introduction of a full scale bidding system for the development of thermal power, the removal and simplification of some administrative procedures and rules to ensure transparency in transactions.

☐ Main Institutional Players

- The Ministry of Economy, Trade and Industry.

☐ Overview

Responsibility for energy policy rests with the government, with The Ministry of Economy, Trade and Industry (METI) takes the lead role. METI has general responsibility for energy policy and is the regulator of the ESI. Within METI, the Agency of Natural Resources and Energy is responsible for the rational development of mineral resources, securing a stable supply of energy, promotion of efficient energy use, and the regulation of the ESI and other energy industries.

METI has a central role in developing the structure of the industry as regards:

- Entry, exit and expansion of utilities and industry assets.
- Co-ordination of utilities.
- Regulation of tariffs and profits.
- Supply reliability, safety and technical regulations.
- Regulation of network access.

Several advisory bodies and political institutions assist METI and co-ordinate the actions of relevant ministries including:

- The Electric Utility Industry Council, a body composed of representatives of industry, the various categories of end-users and other social parties, advises METI on request on all aspects of electricity policy.
- The Electric Power Development Co-ordination Council (EPDCC), chaired by the Prime Minister, settles annual power development plans for the following ten years.

■ Competition

The Japan Fair Trade Commission is the competition authority, responsible for enforcing competition law. The Government of Japan submitted a bill to the Diet on March 21, 2000 that would eliminate the antimonopoly exemption for electricity and other sectors. This will increase the involvement of the Japan Fair Trade Commission in the ESI which, until now, was limited to reviewing and commenting on electricity competition issues, and competition advocacy.

Luxembourg[27]

☐ Regulatory Framework

The industry has some special characteristics. Almost all electricity consumed in Luxembourg is imported and the operation of transmission and distribution is carried out jointly. In this context, there is a regulated third-party access to the grid and end-users and distributors over 100 GWh of annual consumption can choose their supplier. There is no unbundling of accounts or managerial unbundling of system operation; a derogation of the relevant articles of the EU directive has been requested.

☐ Main Institutional Players

■ Ministere d'Energie, Economie et Travaux Publics.
■ Luxembourg Telecommunications Institute.

☐ Overview

The Ministry of Energy, Industry and Public Works regulates the ESI. The Ministry is assisted by the Télécom Regulator (Luxembourg Telecommunications Institute, LTI), an independent agency that has an advisory role on ESI regulatory issues, settling disputes arising from contracts and negotiations or refusal of

---

27. *EU DG XVII: Implementation of the EU Directive by member states.*
http://europa.eu.int/en/comm/dg17/elechome.htm. September1999.
Luxembourg: Loi du 21 mars 1997 sur les télécommunications.

access to the network. Its decisions are open to appeal to the district court. It is also empowered to order fines. Such fines are open to appeal to the administrative tribunal. LTI is consulted on the application of public service obligations, and manages the compensation fund that pays for public service obligations imposed on the industry.

LTI has five members appointed for a renewable three year period. Its operating costs are paid for out of the so-called electricity tax. This is a tax on all electricity consumption primarily intended to finance long-term care insurance for the elderly.

Netherlands[28]

□ Regulatory Framework

There is regulated third-party access to the network. All consumers of more than 2 MW per connection or over 20 GWh of annual consumption can choose their supplier and it is planned that all consumers will be able to choose by 2003. Entry into generation is not subject to specific regulation. A separate Transmission System Operator that is controlled by the state runs system operation. There are no additional provisions concerning the unbundling of accounts except for supply to captive consumers that must be recorded separately.

□ Main Institutional Players

- Ministry of Economic Affairs.
- Competition Authority (NMA), under the authority of the Ministry.
- Network Regulator (DTE), a chamber of NMA.

---

28. EU DG XVII: Implementation of the EU Directive by member states.
http://europa.eu.int/en/comm/dg17/elechome.htm. September1999.
IEA: OECD Regulatory Reform Project: Electricity Chapter of the Netherlands (1998).
OECD: Mini Round Table on Relationship between Regulators and Competition Authorities, Note by the Netherlands. DAFFE. 27 May 1998.

□ Overview

All regulatory responsibilities for electricity fall under the jurisdiction of the Ministry of Economic Affairs. The competition authority (NMA) is under the authority of the Minister and a chamber within the competition authority, the Network Regulator (Dienst Toezicht en Uitvoering Electriciteitswet or DTE) is responsible for the regulation of the electricity network. This approach is unusual and provides an example of the significant variety of institutional approaches to electricity regulation.

The Minister's most important direct roles are to:

- Regulate prices for captive customers, and set out the terms and conditions of supply to these customers through a licensing process.
- Grant dispensations on permitting imports by a customer from a country where a customer would not have a corresponding ability to choose a supplier.
- Approve the privatisation of production or network assets up to the end of 2002, with the possibility of extending this requirement for the networks by four years.

The Minister also has significant indirect influence over the sector. With respect to DTE, the Minister can establish:

- Policy rules with respect to the exercise of DTE's authority.
- Network pricing policy and how investments in networks may be recovered through prices.
- Transmission planning requirements.

DTE regulates the transmission and distribution networks, including:

- Network access prices and other terms of access.
- Review of plans for network expansion.

■ Competition

Competition law applies to the ESI. NMA's general responsibilities are to police anti-competitive behaviour by electricity market participants, mergers, horizontal and vertical agreements. In addition it has specific responsibilities to:

- Review and reach agreement with DTE, on network tariffs and access rules.
- Resolve disputes over network access.

New Zealand[29]

□ Regulatory Framework

The approach to the regulation of network industries is based on the principle that access to essential facilities, including electricity networks, is determined by negotiations between the parties rather than imposition by a regulator. Under this "light-handed" approach there are no price controls or other traditional forms of regulation. Instead, light-handed regulation relies on general competition law, industry-specific information disclosure regulations, which are designed to make transparent the operations of firms with monopoly power; and the threat of heavier-handed regulation, such as price control, if monopoly power is abused.

There is negotiated third-party access to the network, chice of supplier for all consumers and free entry into generation. A voluntary wholesale spot market started operation in 1996. There is ownership unbundling between the competitive functions of generation and retail and transmission and distribution.

□ Main Institutional Players

- Ministry of Economic Development.
- The Commerce Commission (Competition Authority).

---

29. Ministry of Commerce: "New Zealand's electricity Sector". October 1999.
http://www.moc.govt.nz/ers/electric/sector/.
OECD: OECD: Mini Round Table on Relationship between Regulators and Competition Authorities, Note by New Zealand. DAFFE. 27 May 1998.
OECD: Application of Competition Policy to the Electricity Sector. OECD/GD(97)132. 1997.

□ Overview

There are no industry-specific regulators for electricity or other industries, either within government or as autonomous bodies. The main regulatory instruments, apart from general environmental, competition and consumer law, are the information disclosure regulations requiring accounting unbundling of the various electricity functions. These are administered by the relevant Government departments, mainly the Ministry of Economic Development.

The Ministry of Economic Development has general responsibility for energy policy, monitors the ESI and promotes and develops reform proposals. The Ministry for the Environment is responsible for environmental policy and energy efficiency. The specific responsibilities of the Ministry of Economic Development in the area of electricity include:

- The provision of statistics and projections.
- Administering the regulations on disclosure of information by electricity companies.
- Developing regulations and codes of practice relating to the safety, quality and measurement of electricity, and the promotion of health and safety in the electricity sector.
- The registration and ongoing competence of electrical workers.

In October 2000, the government of New Zealand announced plans to reform the regulatory framework. These include a reinforcement of the provisions that would allow government to regulate if industry performance is not satisfactory, a requirement to establish a transmission pricing methodology by the transmission company that will have to be approved by the government and some provisions on electricity prices for small consumers. Overall, the institutions with ESI oversight would remain unchanged but the government powers to regulate the industry would be reinforced.

■ Competition

Competition law fully applies to the ESI. The competition authority is the Commerce Commission, an independent body. The

Commission has been active in all aspects of competition law including:

- The approval of mergers and acquisitions between power companies.

- The authorisation of pricing mechanisms and other rules governing the wholesale market.

- The examination of complaints regarding access to the network and other alleged cases of anti-competitive behaviour.

- Conducting educational programmes to inform and advise electricity companies of their obligations under competition law.

Norway[30]

☐ Regulatory Framework

There is regulated third-party access to the network and all consumers may choose their supplier. Entry into generation is subject to authorisation, particularly as regards the use of hydro resources, which are the main source of electricity in Norway. There is significant trade of electricity with Finland, Sweden and Denmark through Nordpool, a competitive wholesale market. Transmission is owned and operated by an independent publicly owned company and there is accounting unbundling of distribution from generation and electricity sales.

☐ Main Institutional Players

- Ministry of Petroleum and Energy.

- Water Resources and Energy Directorate (NVE).

- The Competition Authority (NCA).

---

30. IEA: Energy Policies of Norway. 1997 Review.
Norway: Electricity Act (30 June 1990).
NVE: Organisation. http://www.nve.no/. 17 March 1999.
OECD: Mini Round Table on Relationship between Regulators and Competition Authorities, Note by Norway. DAFFE. 27 May 1998.

□ Overview

Ultimate responsibility for regulation is with the Ministry of Petroleum and Energy, which is also generally responsible for energy policy. A subordinated ministerial agency, the Water Resources and Energy Directorate (NVE) is responsible for administering water and energy resources. It is intended that NVE should have operational independence in day-to-day affairs. However its decisions can be revised by the Ministry that also acts as court of appeal. The Government is also the owner of Statkraft, the largest electricity producer.

The functions of NVE cover a broad spectrum of regulatory activities and, in particular, network regulation and licensing of electric activities. NVE activities in the electricity sector include:

Regulation of the Network:

■ Setting guidelines for transmission and distribution tariffs and access conditions and monitoring them.

■ Monitoring licence conditions for cross border trade.

Organisation of the Market:

■ Setting guidelines for overall system operation.

Licensing:

■ Issuing licences for the construction and operation of electrical transmission and distribution facilities, windmills, district heating installations and gas fired power plants.

Other:

■ Monitoring all aspects of the evolution of the electricity market such as market structure and performance, regulation, assets and quality of supply and energy efficiency.

NVE employs a staff of 380. Approximately twenty members of the NVE's staff are directly involved in work associated with the regulation of the network.

■ Competition

The Energy Act contains no formal limitations on the scope of the Competition Act. Thus the competition authority (NCA) and the NVE have overlapping competence. According to an informal agreement between the two agencies, the NVE should have sole responsibility for regulating the provision of network services and should have the main responsibility to intervene against anticompetitive behaviour that isnot covered by the prohibitions of the Competition Act. The two agencies issued in 1996 a joint report on the delineation of the competencies of the two agencies that allows for a handling in parallel of merger and anti-competitive behaviour cases, and establishes certain co-ordination and consultation mechanisms between them.

The integration of different national electricity markets has resulted in multilateral co-operation between the regulatory authorities of the NordPool member countries (Finland, Norway, Sweden and, more recently, Denmark) in matters such as approving the rules for the organised markets, transmission tariffs and exchange of information.

Portugal[31]

□ Regulatory Framework

There is a combination of two systems. The Independent System (IS) is open to generators, consumers with choice of supplier, currently those with annual consumption of 9 GWh or higher, small hydro, renewable and co-generation producers. The Public Service System (PSS) includes all consumers not opting for the Independent System, all generation not in the IS, and the transmission and distribution companies. The IS works on the basis

31. AEEG: "Modelli Institutionale a Confronto". In Relazione Annuale sullo Stato dei Servizi E Sull'attivita Svolta. 1998 Report.
ERSE: Relatorio e Contas 1997. Diario da Republica 266/98.
EU DG XVII: Implementation of the EU Directive by member states.
http://europa.eu.int/en/comm/dg17/elechome.htm. September 1999.
Portugal: Decree 187/95 (27 July 1995) Establishing ERSE.

of regulated third-party access to the high and medium voltage networks, free entry into generation subject to a licence, and bilateral contracts between producers and consumers. The PSS is organised on the basis of long-term contracts linking producers and distributors and an obligation to supply to captive consumers. System operation is performed by a separate legal entity. There is also legal unbundling of generation, transmission and distribution activities.

☐ Main Institutional Players

- Ministry of Economic affairs.
- Entidade Reguladora do Sector Electrico (ERSE).
- Competition Council.

☐ Overview

Regulation of the electricity sector is split between the Ministry of Economic Affairs and an independent regulatory agency, the Entidade Reguladora do Sector Electrico (ERSE). The Ministry is responsible for the formulation of general energy policy and regulatory framework, as well as for licensing electric activities.

ERSE is responsible for issuing 4 codes concerning tariffs, commercial relations, network and interconnection access, and dispatch, and for defining consumer eligibility thresholds within the limits established in the law. ERSE is also responsible for setting the regulated prices of electricity and network services. In addition, ERSE serves as a consultative body to the Minister on a limited number of issues including licensing and the monitoring of the electricity market. Quality standards are set jointly by ERSE and the Directorate General of Energy. To conduct these functions, ERSE has powers to require information, and to audit and fine the regulated parties.

ERSE is a collegial body comprising a chairman and two commissioners. They are appointed by government for a renewable five year term and their mandate cannot be revoked. They are subject to an incompatibility regime that prevents them from having any economic interest in the industry. ERSE's decisions can be appealed before an administrative court only, so that the Minister of Economic Affairs cannot repeal its decisions. ERSE decisions are made after listening to both the regulated parties and a consultative body, representing various social interests.

ERSE is financed with a surcharge on "use of system" tariff. Costs in 1997 amounted to nearly 625 million Escudos. In the same year, ERSE had 42 staff.

■ Competition

The Competition Act is, in principle, applicable to the electricity industry and the Competition Council is responsible for its application. However, the PSS, which comprises most of the industry, is primarily subject to the specific electricity regulation.

Spain[32]

☐ Regulatory Framework

There is regulated third-party access to the transmission and distribution network. Consumers of 1 kV and higher can choose their supplier. Entry into generation has been liberalised and is subject to an authorisation procedure. A competitive, non-compulsory wholesale market started operation in 1998. An independent company not controlled by the utilities performs system operation and there is legal and accounting unbundling of transmission and distribution.

☐ Main Institutional Players

- ■ Ministry of Economy.
- ■ National Energy Commission.

32. CNE: Annual Report, 1998.
EU DG XVII: Implementation of the EU Directive by member states.
http://europa.eu.int/en/comm/dg17/elechome.htm. September1999.
IEA: OECD Regulatory Reform Project: Spain. Electricity Chapter. 1999.
Spain: Spanish Electric Power Act, 1998.
Spain: Hydrocarbons Act, 1999.

- Competition Tribunal.
- Autonomous regions.

☐ **Overview**

Regulation of the electricity sector is concentrated at the national level, with some functions carried out by the autonomous communities. The Ministry of Economy is the main regulator of the electricity sector. In addition to having overall policy responsibility for reforms, the Ministry:

- Sets tariffs and charges such as network access tariffs and regulated retail tariffs.
- Allocates revenues among utilities for different cost components such as payments for using domestic coal.
- Regulates the operation of the power market and issues licenses and authorisations to participants.
- Approves transmission projects.
- Establishes minimum quality and safety standards.

Autonomous communities have powers in several areas, including:

- The approval of distribution facilities and other electric facilities "when their use does not affect other regions".
- Issuing authorisations for electricity distribution.
- Legislative powers in the framework of national legislation, including the development of regulations with respect to connection of supply.
- Inspection and disciplinary functions including the enforcement of regulations with respect to quality of service.

The National Energy Commission (Comisión Nacional de Energia) is an independent advisory and dispute resolution agency that deals with the regulation of electricity, gas and oil. The principal functions of the CNE in electricity are to:

- Provide advice and proposals to the Ministry and autonomous regions on electricity matters.

- Arbitrate disputes between agents and solve conflicts relating to access to the network and to the management of the system.
- Approve mergers and acquisitions involving transmission or distribution companies, subject to a review of the decision by the Ministry.
- Monitor the market and report on suspected breaches of the Competition Act.

To carry out these functions, CNE is endowed with powers of inspection and to conduct disciplinary proceedings.

The Board of the CNE is composed of a Chairman and 8 commissioners appointed for a six year mandate that can be renewed once. The Commission and its staff of 118 are partly financed through a levy on electricity tariffs whose size, 1,240 MPTA in 1999, is set by the government. Other financing comes from the oil and gas sectors.

The Spanish Competition Tribunal has the power to apply antitrust rules to the electricity sector particularly in cases of abuse of dominant position and anti-competitive behaviour. In the case of mergers, the Ministry has complete discretion regarding referral to the Tribunal on competition grounds.

Sweden[33]

☐ Regulatory Framework

There is regulated third-party access to the network and all consumers may choose their supplier. Entry into generation is subject to an authorisation procedure that does not contain any energy specific criteria. There is significant trade of electricity with Finland, Norway and Denmark through the nordic competitive

33. EU DG XVII: Implementation of the EU Directive by member states.
http://europa.eu.int/en/comm/dg17/elechome.htm. September1999.
Sweden: Electricity Act (1996).
Sweden: Submission to the IEA of the questionnaire for the In-Depth Review of Swedish Energy Policies.
Some information directly provided by the Swedish Ministry of Industry.

wholesale market (Nordpool). Transmission is owned and operated by an independent publicly owned company and there is legal unbundling of distribution from generation and electricity sales.

□ Main Institutional Players

■ Ministry of Industry, Employment and Communications.

■ Swedish National Energy Administration.

■ Network Authority, part of the Swedish National Energy Administration.

■ Competition Authority.

□ Overview

The lead regulatory responsibility resides with the Ministry of Industry, Employment and Communications. On 1 January 1998, the Swedish National Energy Administration (NEA) was established as a ministerial agency responsible for the main part of the implementation and co-ordination of energy policy. Within NEA, the network authority regulates the network.

The Administration's main task is to promote a safe, efficient and environmentally sustainable supply and use of energy. It does so by supporting research on renewable energy, technology procurement of energy-efficient products and by providing investment support for the development of renewable energy. The Administration also has a supervising function as monitoring authority of the electricity market and provides analyses of the linkages between energy, the environment and economic growth.

The Network Authority, which is part of the NEA, is the specific regulator of the electricity market. It has the task of monitoring network tariffs and other conditions within the monopoly part of the industry. Complaints regarding tariffs from companies or private households are handled by the regulatory authority, which thereby applies the Electricity Act. Its decisions can be appealed to the public administrative court.

The overall regulatory approach is based on limited regulatory intervention. Thus, network tariffs are regulated only indirectly; the network companies manage tariff setting. The network authority monitors tariffs and has the power to accept or reject proposed modifications.

■ Competition

The Competition Authority deals with the application of the competition rules. It also monitors the competitive conditions of production and trading in electricity. It had the special task of following up the electricity market in the first six months after deregulation in 1996.

In addition, the Authority has given the Network Authority assistance in its work of following up the development of market conditions. The Government or the Network Authority regularly invites the Competition Authority to submit its views on reports from the Network Authority. Informal meetings also take place as a complement to formal communication.

Switzerland[34]

☐ Regulatory Framework

The electricity sector comprises a large number of companies, some of them vertically integrated. Competition in generation is not forbidden by law but is prevented in practice by the absence of third-party access obligations. Companies negotiate a tariff for the use of the network. Distributors have an obligation to supply and, in practice, operate as supply monopolies in their exclusive supply areas. There are plans to introduce third-party access to the network as well as to gradually open the market. Initially, this will be for consumers of at least 20 GWh annual consumption and, eventually, for all consumers.

34. IEA: *Energy Policies of Switzerland. 1999 Review.*
Commission de la Concurrence (Switzerland): Rapport Annuel 1998.

□ Main Institutional Players

- Federal Department for Environment, Transport, Energy and Communication.
- Price Surveillance Authority.
- The authorities of the cantons.
- Competition Commission.

□ Overview

At Federal level, the Federal Department for Environment, Transport, Energy and Communication (DETEC) is responsible for energy policy, through the Swiss Federal Office of Energy (SFOE) and the Swiss Agency for Environment, Forests and Landscape (SAEFL). The Ministry has overall regulatory and administrative power and is specifically responsible for issuing licenses for electricity exports. Many regulatory powers are managed by the cantons.

At Federal level the Price Surveillance Authority, an agency of the Swiss government, is in charge of price monitoring in electricity supply and other industries. It comprises 14 members. The Government nominates the head of the Authority. Prices for large consumers are set by the utilities. Electricity prices for other consumers are set by the utilities or by local authorities. Consumers can complain to the Authority. In cases where public authorities approve or set prices, it can only issue recommendations which utilities are not obliged to follow.

The cantons have authority for all aspects of energy policy not regulated at the Federal level including the regulation of distribution. They are also responsible for the implementation of Federal policy, setting taxes and charges on electricity companies, approving siting procedures for most electricity plants, and they have jurisdiction over the use of water.

■ Competition

Competition law applies in principle to the ESI but no significant cases have been reported. The application of the Act is the duty of the Competition Commission, an independent federal authority. The Commission has been an active player in the discussion on the proposed reform of the electricity sector.

Turkey[35]

□ Regulatory Framework

Until recently the industry was dominated by two state-owned enterprises – TEAS in generation and TEDAS in distribution – that report to the Ministry of Energy and Natural Resources. In addition, there are independent power producers who can be allowed by the Ministry to sell electricity directly to customers at a negotiated price. There are also a number of private distribution companies. Prices are set by the two main public companies and approved by the Ministry. There is no statutory market opening; however during the course of the privatisation programme, the competition authority has required that the market be open to end-users of 1 MW capacity or more.

□ Main Institutional Players

- Ministry of Energy and Natural Resources (MENR).
- State Planning Organisation.
- Competition Board.

□ Overview

The Ministry of Energy and Mineral Resources (MENR) has most regulatory responsibilities. Every year, TEAS and TEDAS investment plans are submitted to the MENR, which has to approve them. Programmes are then submitted to the State Planning Organisation (SPO) which discusses them with the two companies. The State Planning Organisation evaluates the needs of the electricity sector for new investments and has the final say in investment decisions. MENR grants permission to autoproducers. Electricity tariffs are not to be

35. IEA: Energy Policies of Turkey. 1997 Review.
OECD: Annual Report on Competition Policy and Law in Turkey. 1998.

formally set by the administration but prices set by TEAS and TEDAS have been influenced by government policies. Private generators can be allowed by MENR to sell electricity directly to customers at a negotiated price. MENR is also in charge of the planning, design and building of hydro plants as well as flood protection, irrigation and land drainage works. Once the plants are commissioned, responsibility for their operation is handed over to TEAS.

There are plans to establish a Supreme Board of Energy that will assume some regulatory responsibilities including those related to tariffs, eligibility of end-users and unbundling of distribution from retail activities. The precise status of this new organisation has not yet been established.

■ Competition

Competition law applies to the electricity sector. The Turkish Competition Board enforces competition law. It has been active in approving acquisitions of electricity undertakings in the context of the privatisation programme. The approval of the acquisition has been made conditional on the modification of certain sale conditions, such as exclusivity rights on certain distribution zones and fixed electricity prices.

United Kingdom[36]

□ Regulatory Framework

In England and Wales there is regulated third-party access to the network and full consumer choice. All electricity trade is

---

36. Department of Trade and Industry (UK): A Fair Deal for Consumers. Modernising the Framework for Utility Regulation. 1998.
Department of Trade and Industry Web site. February 2000.
EU DG XVII: Implementation of the EU Directive by member states.
http://europa.eu.int/en/comm/dg17/elechome.htm. September 1999.
IEA: Energy Policies of the UK. 1998 Review.
OECD: Mini Roundtable on Relationship between Regulators and Competition Authorities. Note by the UK. Daffe/CLP/WD(98)23. 1998.
Offer: Annual Report. 1997.
Ofgem: Web Site. February 2000.
UK: Competition Bill. 1998.
UK: Electricity Act. 1989.

currently conducted through a mandatory competitive wholesale market but bilateral trade outside the pool will be allowed shortly. The regulation of industry is conducted primarily through the licensing of generation, transmission and supply. Entry into generation is subject to an authorisation procedure that may take into account energy specific criteria. There is an independent transmission company that is also responsible for system operation. Distribution is unbundled and there is a prohibition on distribution companies to engage in production with more than 15% of their supply. Scotland has a similar framework but the market is made up of two fully vertically integrated electricity companies. These companies are subject to a management unbundling obligation. In Northern Ireland there is no market opening. There are four major generation companies and a single vertically integrated transmission, distribution and supply company.

□ Main Institutional Players

- Department of Trade and Industry (Ministry).
- Office of Gas and Electricity Regulation (OFGEM), the independent regulator in England and Wales and Scotland.
- Competition Commission.

□ Overview

The Department of Trade and Industry (DTI) is the responsible Ministry with overall supervisory and executive functions on energy policy. DTI has a leading role in the ongoing review of energy regulation and in pressing forward with legislative reform of energy regulation. The consent or agreement of DTI's Secretary of State is required for key regulatory decisions such as the licensing of generators, transmission and electricity supply companies. Alternatively the Ministry may issue licences with the consent of the Director General of Electricity Supply.

There is a separate regulatory office for Northern Ireland.

■ OFGEM

The Office of Gas and Electricity Regulation (OFGEM) is the main regulatory authority. OFGEM was formed early in 1999 by combining the functions of the former Office of Gas Supply (OFGAS) and the Office of Electricity Regulation (OFFER). In the ESI, OFGEM is, in particular, responsible for all price regulation and issuing and monitoring of licenses, in collaboration with DTI, as described above. The Office board comprises one person, the Director General of Electricity Supply. Its duties are to ensure that all reasonable demands for electricity are met, that license holders are able to finance their licensed activities, to promote competition in the generation and supply of electricity, to protect the interests of electricity customers in respect of prices charged, to ensure continuity of supply and the quality of services provided, and to promote efficiency and economy on the part of licensees in supplying and transmitting electricity.

The specific functions of the Director General of Electricity Supply are:

Licenses:

- Granting licenses to persons who wish to supply, transmit or generate electricity under a general authority from the Secretary of State.
- Enforcing the conditions of licenses and certain provisions of the Electricity Act.
- Considering what changes may be required to licenses issued under the Act, including periodically reviewing those provisions which embody price controls.
- Investigating complaints about licensees.

Consumer Protection:

- Resolving certain types of disputes between customers and public electricity suppliers.
- Setting Standards of Performance for aspects of customer service and promoting the efficient use of electricity.

- Establishing and maintaining arrangements for the representation of customers.
- Fixing and publishing maximum charges for reselling electricity.
- Publishing information and advice for the benefit of customers with regulated tariffs.

Network Access:

- Determining connection and use of system agreements under which suppliers have access to the distribution systems of the regional electricity companies and the National Network.

Defense of Competition and Monitoring of Industry:

- Overseeing the development of competition and the activities of licensees and referring any anti-competitive practices to the Competition Commission.
- Keeping under review developments concerning the ESI.

The Director General is appointed for a period not exceeding five years and can be re-appointed. As of 1997, Offer employed 233 staff. Its running costs in the financial year ending March 1997 were around UK Pounds 13 million. As a non-Ministerial Government Department, OFGEM's funds are voted by Parliament and accounted for each year through the Appropriation Account, which is audited by the National Audit Office. OFGEM's costs are recovered through the annual licence fees paid by licensees. The licence fees are based upon an objective measure of market activity, namely megawatt hours generated, transmitted, distributed or supplied, according to type of license.

■ Competition

Competition law fully applies to the ESI. The Director General of Electricity Supply has concurrent powers with the Director General of Fair Trading in respect of cases concerning anti-competitive behaviour. Merger cases are under the exclusive jurisdiction of the Director General of Fair Trading, who advises DTI's Secretary of State on whether to clear the transaction; or refer the transaction to the Competition Commission; or accept undertakings in lieu of a reference to the Commission. The Director General of Electricity Supply has, on at least one occasion, formally and publicly threatened to make a monopoly reference. Under a Concordat between OFFER and the Office of Fair Trading, the former provides advice to the latter on mergers, acquisitions or take-over bids involving licensees.

United States[37]

□ Regulatory Framework

At the Federal level, there is regulated third-party access to the network, entry into generation is open to all parties and generators can compete to sell electricity. The utilities are often vertically integrated but transmission assets are in many cases under the control of an independent system operator or other form of regional transmission organisation. There has been considerable legislative debate on introducing full consumer choice and federal legislation is expected. There is already full consumer choice in over a half of the fifty states.

□ Main Institutional Players

- Department of Energy (DOE).
- Federal Energy Regulatory Commission (FERC).
- State Public Utilities Commissions.
- Department of Justice (DOJ).
- Federal trade Commission (FTC).

---

37. *California: Public Utilities Code. Updated February 2000.*
CPUC: Web page. November 1999.
FERC: Annual Report 1997.
FERC: Congressional Budget Request FY 1999.
FERC: Web site. January 2000.
IEA: Energy Policies of the US. 1998 Review.
OECD: Regulatory Reform in the US. 1999.
OECD: Mini Roundtable on Relationship between Regulators and Competition Authorities. Note by the US. Daffe/CLP/WD(98)23. 1998.

☐ Overview

Regulatory and legislative powers are divided between the states and the federal government. Inter-state commerce falls into federal competence, whereas intra-state commerce is a state domain. In practice, this means that wholesale[38] electricity sales and a large part of transmission services fall within federal competence while retail sales and distribution services are regulated by the states.

Several federal bodies address inter-state trade. The DOE is the ministry responsible for general energy policy and, specifically, for energy security, environmental quality, and science and technology related to energy. In particular, DOE has been active in promoting regulatory reform in the US ESI and pressing forward with new legislation, such as the 1998 Comprehensive Electricity Competition Plan.

The main regulatory institution at federal level is FERC. In addition, every state has a state regulatory commission which oversees all regulated industries, including electricity, gas, telecommunications, and railroads. As an example, the California Public Utilities Commission is considered below. State governments retain some regulatory powers such as those related to siting and construction permits. However, the state regulatory commission exercises most regulatory powers.

■ Federal Energy Regulatory Commission (FERC)

FERC is an independent regulatory agency within the Department of Energy. It regulates electricity and hydroelectric power, as well as the natural gas and oil transportation industries. FERC has jurisdiction over activities and transactions in interstate commerce.

In the ESI, FERC sets industry wide rules for electricity sales and transmission in interstate commerce. FERC is specifically responsible for:

---

38. The concepts of wholesale and retail electricity sales are discussed in Energy Policies of the US. 1998 Review.

- Approving rates for wholesale electric sales of electricity and transmission in interstate commerce for private utilities, power marketers, power pools, power exchanges and independent system operators.
- Reviewing rates set by the federal power marketing administrations.
- Ordering the provision of transmission services upon request.
- Overseeing mergers and acquisitions.
- Reviewing utility pooling and co-ordination agreements.
- Monitoring and overseeing the industry, including the issue of certain stock and debt securities, assuming obligations and liabilities, and reviewing officer and director positions held by top officials in utilities and certain other firms with which they do business.
- Providing certification for qualifying small power production and co-generation facilities, and approving certain exemptions to the wholesale generator status.

FERC was created on October 1, 1977, to replace the Federal Power Commission. It is made up of five members who serve staggered five-year terms, are appointed by the President and confirmed by the Senate. No more than three commissioners may belong to the same political party. The chairman, designated by the President, serves as the Commission's administrative head. As of 1998, FERC had approximately 1400 staff. Some 470 staff worked in electric power activities and another 389 in hydropower.

The Commission recovers all of its costs from regulated industries through fees and annual charges. Specifically, FERC collects revenue for the Treasury through fees on the industry but is actually funded through annual appropriations from Congress. The fees collected are equal to the appropriated budget. This arrangement allows Congress to retain oversight and budgetary approval while passing costs on to the users through fees. The budget for 1998 was of the order of US $162 million, of which some US $52 million were allocated to electric power activities.

■ California Public Utilities Commission (CPUC)

The responsibilities of the public utilities commissions vary from state to state. California is reviewed here as an example. CPUC regulates the rates and services of investor-owned companies in electric, natural gas, water, steam, sewer, pipeline, local telephone and transportation. It does not regulate municipal or district-owned utilities, or so-called mutual water companies. CPUC's jurisdiction in the ESI covers distribution activities and retail sales. The state government is specifically responsible for siting[39] and construction permits that are given under the authority of the Energy Commission, an agency of the State government.

Under the Californian Public Utilities Code, CPUC has a general mandate to supervise and regulate all utilities within the state and, in the context of electricity restructuring, to develop rules and other measures needed to implement reform. CPUC specific functions in the power industry are:

■ Setting rates for electricity and distribution services.

■ Regulating service standards.

■ Monitoring utility operations for safety.

All may involve public hearings. In all formal proceedings, one of the CPUC Commissioners and an Administrative Law Judge are assigned to guide the case upon written request of a party.

The Commission consists of five commissioners appointed by the governor, and approved by the senate, for terms of six years. Commissioners' terms are staggered to ensure that experienced members are always present on the panel. One of the five is elected annually to serve as president of the Commission. The president chairs the decision-making meetings and other formal sessions, and assigns cases among the members. Three types of proceedings – applications, complaints, and investigations – are used by the CPUC to reach a decision. The five commissioners as

---

39. In this respect, California is somewhat special. In other states, the siting authority typically resides with the PUC and not with the State government.

a whole make all final decisions on policy and procedures. Any decision or order of the Commission is subject to both administrative and judicial review.

The commissioners appoint an executive director responsible for the day-to-day operations of the agency. The executive office and nine divisions, each headed by a director, carry out the work of the Commission. The staff includes more than 800 people, including approximately 72 that work for the Energy Division.

CPUC is primarily funded with fees paid by the utilities it regulates. Some additional revenue comes from fees charged for services provided by the Commission. Fees are set so as to equate the total budget approved by the State Legislature. Budget for the regulation of utilities, excluding transportation and other items, for fiscal year 1999-2000 was approximately US$ 66 Million.

■ Competition

The antitrust agencies – DOJ and FTC – and FERC have overlapping jurisdiction with respect to mergers among electric utilities. FERC reviews mergers under a public interest standard. This differs from the standard under competition law which prohibits mergers, the effect of which "may be substantially to lessen competition" in any relevant market. Although FERC is not bound to use antitrust principles when considering a merger, its policy is to primarily focus on the competitive effects of mergers. The antitrust agencies can sue to block a merger approved by FERC, and FERC can refuse to approve a merger on which DOJ and the FTC have taken no action. Proposed Federal electricity legislation does not contain antitrust immunity provisions.

The antitrust agencies' role in electric power to date has been mostly that of advocate and advisor, both because of the relatively early stage of reform and the statutory role of FERC in reviewing mergers of utilities engaged in the interstate sale and transmission of electricity.

CONCLUSIONS

The Emergence of Independent Regulation

■ Independent Regulatory Agencies are Increasingly Common in the ESI

The most significant change in the institutional framework of the ESI and other network industries is the increasing number of independent regulatory agencies. Many of these agencies have been created in step with market reforms. Formally independent ESI regulators are now active in Australia, Canada, Denmark, Finland, France, Ireland, Italy, Portugal, Sweden, the United Kingdom and the United States. There are independent agencies with an advisory role in Belgium, Luxembourg and Spain and one is planned in Greece. In addition, a number of countries have set up ministerial offices subordinate to the line ministry but largely autonomous in the day-to-day management of regulation. This is the approach in Hungary, the Netherlands and Norway. In the remaining countries examined – Austria, Germany, Japan, New Zealand, Switzerland, and Turkey – all regulatory tasks are conducted by government.

Independent regulatory agencies are common in countries with a larger degree of market opening and regulated third-party access. Line ministries tend to retain most regulatory powers in countries where market opening is limited. In countries where access to the network is negotiated, such as Germany and New Zealand, ministries remain the main regulatory authority, but their role in day-to-day regulation is naturally limited.

The choice between an independent regulatory agency and a ministerial agency can be related to the objectives of reform. Ministerial agencies arise in response to managerial challenges. Market-oriented reforms generally require countries to allocate more resources to regulatory tasks and to develop new regulatory competencies. Both types of agency assemble these expanded regulatory resources into homogeneous and more or less autonomous units to provide better management and control. Independent regulatory agencies are also a response to these managerial challenges. In addition, they strengthen the neutrality or independence of regulatory decisions. Independent advisory bodies have the autonomy of an independent regulator but no decision-making authority.

■ "Strong" Regulatory Agencies are Found in Countries with a Strong Unbundling Policy

Independent regulatory agencies diverge widely in their powers and independence. This variation is partly explained by the regulatory framework in which the agency is set up to operate. Restructuring or "unbundling" policies in the ESI are common in countries with a "strong" regulatory agency while market reform without restructuring is more frequently observed in countries in which independent regulation plays a lesser role. This pattern seems to reflect the larger demand for independent regulatory activity in an unbundled ESI.

Some countries restructured the ESI at the time of introducing competition. Restructuring measures include vertical unbundling of competitive activities, such as generation and end-user supply, and horizontal divestiture to reduce market power or to facilitate comparability among distribution companies. Australia, Italy, New Zealand, the UK and the US provide examples of this approach. Strong regulatory agencies separated from the ministry and endowed with relatively large regulatory powers are common in countries following this strategy, such as Australia, Italy, the UK, the US and, still at a planning stage, Canada.

On the other hand, relatively large regulatory powers have remained with the ministry in most of the countries that had not restructured the ESI at the time of opening the market. Sweden, Norway, Finland, Germany, Denmark, the Netherlands, and Spain provide examples.

To summarise, the choice of regulatory organisations is not arbitrary. Institutional and regulatory frameworks need to be consistent and, in practice, regulatory organisations seem to be adapted to the particular regulatory needs of each system.

What do Independent Regulators have in Common?

Independent regulatory agencies are largely country-specific. There are important differences in the objectives, powers and independence of agencies. However, some key elements are shared by most agencies. This least common denominator suggests a blueprint from which ESI regulatory agencies are designed and adapted to national circumstances.

■ Objectives

The role of independent ESI regulators is largely concentrated in two interrelated areas. One is monopoly control. Most regulatory agencies are responsible for the control of prices and access in the monopolistic segments of the ESI – transmission and distribution – and with avoiding any anti-competitive impact of these segments on generation and supply. The other is consumer protection. Regulatory agencies often have responsibility for end-user tariffs and other conditions. However, some agencies have a more general mission to promote efficiency in the ESI, including oversight of the competitive activities.

■ Jurisdiction

Regulatory agencies in the ESI generally deal with economic regulation only. Social regulation is the responsibility of other authorities. As an exception to this rule, the UK launched in 1998 a review of the role of regulators that aimed to shift the emphasis of their activity from efficiency towards distributional issues. The government proposed changing the primary statutory duty of regulators to one of consumer protection, including dealing with "fuel poverty" and other social objectives.

Competition law is not the primary responsibility of ESI regulators except in Australia, where the competition authority is also the ESI independent regulator. However, ESI regulators often perform some supporting functions for the application of competition policy, such as monitoring, providing information and advice or bringing cases before the competition authority. In the US, the regulator has concurrent jurisdiction with the antitrust authority in merger cases.

■ Industry Coverage

The same institutions that regulate electricity are often also in charge of regulating gas and other primary energies. Electricity and gas are regulated by the same institution in Australia, Canada, Italy, Spain, the UK and the US. This is consistent with ministries that also cover both electricity and gas. This pattern of association of electricity and gas reflects significant and growing interdependencies between the two industries, such as the increasing use of gas for power generation and the integration of gas and electricity firms. It also reflects the fact that both are network industries facing similar regulatory issues, like access to the network, and subject to a similar regulatory approach (both industries are being deregulated). In countries where the regulatory approach to gas and electricity differs, with only one industry open to competition, establishing a multi-industry regulator seems more difficult.

■ Decision-making

A commission governs a majority of regulatory agencies, the exceptions being Finland and the UK where there is a one-person regulatory board. However, the Utilities Bill in the UK will establish a collegial board for the regulatory agency. The issue of whether collegial or one-person regulatory boards should be preferred was discussed in Chapter 2.

■ Appointment of Regulators

Appointments are for a fixed term, between three and seven years, except in Finland and Sweden, where the appointment is for an indefinite period. Casual observation indicates that, with few exceptions, stakeholders are not appointed as regulators but this does not seem to obey formal rules.

■ Independence Safeguards

Formal independence safeguards generally include the non-revocability of appointments except in extreme circumstances, such as serious misconduct or insanity, a separate budget, managerial autonomy, and a stable source of financing. However, the actual source of financing varies. Costs can be recovered either from end-users, network users or licence holders.

■ Functions

The functions of independent agencies vary. However, the regulation of the monopoly elements of the ESI is typically allocated to the independent agency when there is one. The regulation of transmission is a core activity of most independent regulatory agencies. Portugal, where transmission is regulated by the ministry, is the exception. Another common activity of independent regulators is the regulation of end-user tariffs.

To carry out these tasks, regulatory agencies are typically responsible for monitoring market conditions, compiling and auditing company information and pursuing and penalising misconduct.

The more technical aspects of regulation, such as the rules for system operation, are frequently left to industry bodies, while the more strategic aspects of regulation and legislation are conducted by legislative bodies and government. In the US, there has been an increase in legislative activity by the states in areas that were traditionally handled by the Public Utilities Commissions. Also, in some states such as California, stakeholders have taken a leading role in developing operational rules.

In federal countries, there is a split of regulatory functions between the federal and the state or provincial regulators, with the latter typically being responsible for the regulation of retail markets, including distribution and retail supply activities. This is the case in Australia, Canada and the US. The split of regulatory powers reflects the local nature of distribution and retail supply services versus the system-wide dimension of transmission and generation.

■ Process and Appeals

The procedures of regulatory agencies in IEA countries show significant similarities. These include:

- A decision-making process, typically including an obligation to conduct hearings and consultations with affected parties and to make decisions reasoned and public.

- An appeals mechanism, typically establishing that either an administrative court or an ordinary court of justice is the appeals body.

- Mechanisms to make these institutions accountable, typically including an obligation to submit a report of activities to the parliament or other political body, and some form of auditing and control of performance by the relevant administrative body.

Policy Implications

Regulatory institutions in the ESI are changing in step with the development of new regulatory frameworks. Institutional change reflects the industry's adaptation to a new regulatory environment that is characterised by open electricity markets, new regulatory needs such as transmission pricing, increasing regionalisation and increasing links between industries.

The allocation of powers and responsibilities to different organisations makes objectives more explicit and decisions more transparent in each area of public intervention. It also provides for a framework that supports neutrality in regulatory decisions. There is, however, no institutional "free-lunch". The co-existence of several institutions with jurisdiction over the ESI creates complexity which spawns increased co-ordination among the various authorities involved and, possibly, greater compliance costs to the regulated parties. Developing co-ordination mechanisms in the increasingly complex institutional setting of the ESI is a key condition of effective reform.

The multiplication of organisations also raises concerns about the efficiency of the public sector. Bureaucracies are costly, and tend to grow and self-perpetuate. Thus, it is essential that regulatory institutions be examined over time and that their role and resources be continuously adapted. A key challenge in this regard is to find the appropriate balance between general energy policy, industry-specific regulation and competition policy. The relative weight of each of these policies is gradually changing as competition in electricity markets progresses. The allocation of resources to different policy areas may need to be adjusted in response.

In periodically reviewing the institutional setting, the changing boundaries of the electricity industry must be taken into account. The need for harmonisation across the gas and electricity industries and across trading areas will continue to put pressure on regulatory institutions. The scope of sector regulators may need to change to cope with these structural changes as has been the case with the merger of electricity and gas regulators in some countries. Further change can be expected in this very dynamic setting.

Most independent regulatory agencies share a number of characteristics. These common elements provide a blueprint for the design of new agencies. This blueprint is, however, incomplete as regulatory agencies differ widely on a number of issues. Designing regulatory mechanisms will benefit greatly from the international experience.

Box 2

A Brief Annotated Bibliography

The economic and political economy aspects of regulatory institutions are discussed in a variety of sources.

An introductory overview is provided by B. Tenenbaun in **"Regulation: What the Prime Minister needs to know"** (The Electricity Journal, March 1996).

A more detailed and specific introduction can be found in **"Utility Regulators"** by W. Smith (http://www.worldbank.org/html/fpd/notes/ competition.htm, 1997), including a detailed discussion of managerial and organisational issues.

Funding and related financing issues are discussed in **"Regulating Infrastructure"** (Economic Notes, Country Dept. I, World Bank, September 1995) by W. Smith and B. Shin.

A comprehensive overview with a focus in the US can be found in **"Economics of Regulation and Antitrust"** (MIT Press, 1998) by Viscusi, Vernon and Harrington, chapters 2 and 10.

The relationship between economic and social regulators and the logic underlying the choice of institutions in the energy sector (particularly in the UK) are discussed in **"Energy and the Environment: the Institutional Framework"** (February 1998) by Yarrow and Keyworth (http://www.rcep.org.uk/studies/energy/98-6066/yarrow.html).

Several contributions consider the costs and benefits of alternative institutional arrangements.

Transparency in regulation is discussed by A. Brown in **"Transparency in Regulated Industries: Elements and Importance"** (Harvard Electricity Policy Group, http://ksgwww.harvard.edu/hepg/, 1966).

The role of regulatory institutions as a means of restraining political opportunism is discussed in P. Spiller's **"Institutions and**

Commitment" (In Industrial and Corporate Change, Vol 3, No. 2, Oxford University Press, 1996) and the references therein.

An alternative view, based on the idea that two (or more) regulators can be more effective than one is developed by J.J. Laffont and D. Martimort in **"Separation of Regulators against Collusive Behavior"** (Rand Journal of Economics, Vol 30, No. 2, 1999).

A common source of inspiration for these more theoretical studies is the concept of regulatory capture. A survey of this and other related political economy issues can be found in **"Economic Perspectives on the Politics of Regulation"** (Handbook of Industrial Organization, Elsevier, 1989) by R. Noll.

The discussion paper **"Best Practice Utility Regulation"** issued by the Australian Utility Regulators Forum in July 1999 provides some interesting insights on practical issues.

These issues are further discussed in **"Developments in Best-Practice Regulation: Principles, Processes and Performance"** written by Prof. S. Berg and published in the July 2000 issue of the Electricity Journal.

References on national approaches are provided in the endnotes to chapter 3.

Box 3

Regulatory Institutions on the Internet

Most regulatory institutions can be reached through the Internet. The International Forum for Utility Regulation of the World Bank maintains a comprehensive list of ministries and regulatory agencies for electricity supply and other industries covering the whole world. The International Directory of Utility Regulatory Institutions can be consulted at:

http://www.worldbank.org/html/fpd/psd/ifur/directory/index.html

Order Form

**INTERNATIONAL
ENERGY AGENCY**

**ORGANISATION
FOR ECONOMIC
CO-OPERATION
AND DEVELOPMENT**

OECD PARIS CENTRE

Tel: (+33-01) 45 24 81 47
Fax: (+33-01) 45 24 19 50
E-mail: sales@oecd.org

OECD BONN CENTRE

Tel: (+49-228) 959 12 15
Fax: (+49-228) 959 12 18
E-mail: bonn.contact@oecd.org

OECD MEXICO CENTRE

Tel: (+52-5) 280 12 09
Fax: (+52-5) 280 04 80
E-mail: mexico.contact@oecd.org

*Please send your order
by mail, fax, or e-mail
to your nearest
IEA sales point
or through
the online service:
www.oecd.org/bookshop*

OECD TOKYO CENTRE

Tel: (+81-3) 3586 2016
Fax: (+81-3) 3584 7929
E-mail: center@oecdtokyo.org

OECD WASHINGTON CENTER

Tel: (+1-202) 785-6323
Toll-free number for orders:
(+1-800) 456-6323
Fax: (+1-202) 785-0350
E-mail: washington.contact@oecd.org

I would like to order the following publications

PUBLICATIONS	ISBN	QTY	PRICE*	TOTAL
☐ **Regulatory Institutions in Liberalised Electricity Markets**	92-64-18583-6		$75	
☐ Competition in Electricity Markets	92-64-18559-3		$75	
☐ Regulatory Reform: European Gas	92-64-18558-5		$75	
☐ Electricity Reform: Power Generation Costs and Investment	92-64-16961-X		$50	
☐ Electricity Market Reform - An IEA Handbook	92-64-16187-2		$50	
☐ World Energy Outlook 2000	92-64-18513-5		$150	
☐ Electric Power Technology - *Opportunities and Challenges of Competition*	92-64-17133-9		$40	
☐ Energy Policies of IEA Countries – 2000 Review (Compendium)	92-64-18565-8		$120	
			TOTAL	

*Postage and packing fees will be added to each order.

DELIVERY DETAILS

Name _____ Organisation _____
Address _____

Country _____ Postcode _____
Telephone _____ Fax _____

PAYMENT DETAILS

☐ I enclose a cheque payable to IEA Publications for the sum of US$ _____ or FF _____

☐ Please debit my credit card (tick choice). ☐ Access/Mastercard ☐ Diners ☐ VISA ☐ AMEX

Card no: ⌞_⌟_⌞_⌟_⌞_⌟_⌞_⌟_⌞_⌟_⌞_⌟_⌞_⌟_

Expiry date: ⌞_⌟_⌞_⌟_⌞_⌟ Signature: _____

Visit our Web site: www.iea.org

IEA PUBLICATIONS, 9, rue de la Fédération, 75739 PARIS Cedex 15
Photo PIX - Printed in France by Chirat
(61 01 01 1 P) ISBN 92-64-185836 2001